Emotional Incest in Group Psychotherapy

Emotional Incest in Group Psychotherapy

A Conspiracy of Silence

Robert S. Pepper

ROWMAN & LITTLEFIELD
Lanham • Boulder • New York • London

Published by Rowman & Littlefield
A wholly owned subsidiary of The Rowman & Littlefield Publishing Group, Inc.
4501 Forbes Boulevard, Suite 200, Lanham, Maryland 20706
www.rowman.com

16 Carlisle Street, London W1D 3BT, United Kingdom

British Library Cataloguing in Publication Information Available

Library of Congress Cataloging-in-Publication Data

Pepper, Robert S., 1947- , author.
Emotional incest in group psychotherapy : a conspiracy of silence / Robert S. Pepper.
p. cm.
Includes bibliographical references and index.
ISBN 978-1-4422-4401-6 (cloth : alk. paper) — ISBN 978-1-4422-4402-3 (ebook)
I. Title. [DNLM: 1. Psychotherapy, Group. 2. Interpersonal Relations. 3. Psychotherapeutic Processes. WM 430]
RC480.5
616.89'14—dc23
2014027479

∞™ The paper used in this publication meets the minimum requirements of American National Standard for Information Sciences Permanence of Paper for Printed Library Materials, ANSI/NISO Z39.48-1992.

Printed in the United States of America

To my parents, Alex and Lillian Pepper,
whose love of learning inspired me to teach.

Contents

Preface

I have called the first part of the title "Emotional Incest in Group Psychotherapy" to distinguish this book from the work of others like Gabbard & Lester (1995), who focus on sexual enactments in individual treatment. Emotionally incestuous relationships in group psychotherapy blur the boundary between therapy and not-therapy. Group members often experience these relationships as too close for comfort. Under some circumstances, they have been prohibited by professional organizations (Clinical Social Work Federation 1997, American Psychological Association, 2002).

Although no physical contact takes place, the non-sexual blurring of boundaries in group psychotherapy opens the door to the intrusion of unconscious and largely uncontrolled elements of the subjective countertransference, which are nonetheless undermining of the emotional, and even at times the physical, well-being of patients. This constitutes an abuse of power.

The second part of the title, "A Conspiracy of Silence," refers to and emphasizes the clandestine nature of such enactments. Incest is always a secret. It is the secretive nature of boundary violations in analytic group therapy, be they sexual or not, that are my concern here.

There is often a tacit collusion[1] between group leaders and members not to talk about the compromised treatment. It is not so much that these enactments are hidden, although sometimes they are, but that their pernicious consequences for the treatment are not addressed. Often, in a blurred boundary treatment environment, the leader's directive to "say everything" is precluded by the unspoken directive not to. This is a maleficent component of blurred treatment boundaries because of its destabilizing effect on the therapy.

I have written this book for both personal and professional reasons. My experience with complicated dual-role relationships as a patient/trainee with my own group therapist and with colleagues, fellow students, fellow supervisees, and friends who were also my fellow group therapy members at an analytic institute were the initial impetus to research the impact of these relationships in treatment; subsequently my interest broadened to include other altered frame environments as well.

I began my own group therapy in my mid-twenties, well before I was a group therapist myself, because I wanted to understand my part in failed romantic relationships. What started off as group treatment in a secure frame setting—that is, one in which the leader and members were solely known to each other in their professional relationships, and members were known to each other only in the treatment group and were otherwise anonymous to each other— morphed into something quite different once I began training as a group leader. It was simultaneously one of the best and worst things that had ever happened to me. It was truly a mixed blessing.

My journey to becoming a group psychotherapist was actually a combination of a series of blunders and good luck. But then again, I don't think any kid says to himself, "I want to be a group therapist when I grow up"; a fireman or doctor maybe, but not a group therapist. I have come to think of the driving force behind this project as *bashert*—the Yiddish word for fate. It has felt like it was my destiny to write this book.

From having had my dream of becoming a college professor deferred by the Vietnam War, which led into public school teaching in a ghetto neighborhood, which forever changed the course of my life, to the good fortune of finding mentors who taught me both what to do and (unwittingly) what not to do as group leaders, to academic teachers who, at different phases of my intellectual development, guided me in ways that I never would have considered, to meeting people who wrote about the social structure of training institutes long before I had any interest in or understanding of the subject, to finding important books in the $1 discount rack on the street outside the Strand Bookstore in Greenwich Village, books that helped me formulate my thinking on the subject, to having had my group therapist encourage and support me in becoming a group therapist and training at his institute—who then also became my supervisor/colleague/teacher/administrator/buddy—who then told me his own dreams, dreams that shed light on his unconscious struggle with me—to ultimately finding a therapist and a supervisor who both were unaffiliated with that institute and who both had a very clear sense of boundaries and who helped me to unravel the quagmire that I was in—all seemed like pieces of a puzzle that have fatefully come together.

In addition to providing me with a stimulating and gratifying career as a group therapist, my journey has also provided me with a lifetime of material to write about. Originally schooled as a sociologist, I looked at interactions at the institute where I was trained from the perspective of a dynamic social system rather than solely in terms of individual motivation and personality, as many of my colleagues did—colleagues whose graduate training was mostly in psychology. I saw, and still see, things from the point of view of latent and manifest consequences in social interaction. When I was finally able to extricate myself from what was, in the end, a torturous mess, I wanted to understand what caused my great emotional turmoil (which I did not recognize at the time were symptoms of an induced narcissistic transference reaction), and I wanted to pass on that understanding to the community of group therapists, to their patients, and to the community at large.

My hope is that, in the telling of my experiences, and what I have observed about fellow group therapists, others in comparable compromised treatment settings may be helped to avoid a similar ordeal, and to help other professionals consider the possibility that some treatment impasses may be related to the treatment frame itself.

At the risk of sounding dramatic, during my darkest hours I thought that I had to be strong and to hold on to life first for my young daughter and also to someday be able to tell my story. I believe that I survived in part to alert the profession to the danger of hubris, the thinking on the part of some senior leaders who believe that they are immune from the dangers of frame alterations simply by virtue of their brilliance.

The following account took place during the time that I was in group treatment with a leader who was simultaneously my individual therapist, supervisor, teacher, and colleague at a mental health clinic where I worked as a staff therapist and he was also my wife's individual and group therapist. I would never again be enmeshed with a therapist as I was then.

At the time that this occurred, I was in my early thirties and had been in treatment with this clinician, Dr. K., for more than ten years. The treatment began in a secure frame setting, but changed into a complicated dual relationship after I started training with him at the analytic institute that was affiliated with the clinic where we both worked. The story begins after I had learned that, after several years of remission, my father's cancer had returned with a vengeance.

I panicked when told that his illness had advanced to stage 4 prostate cancer, a terminal diagnosis. I was scared of losing the father that I never had. Stage 4 cancer was a death sentence; it was a curse for him to die so young. I knew that, at age 66, he didn't have much time left. His final months were agony.

The night that I told the group about my father's final death-sentence diagnosis, Dr. K. offered me a solution that seemed like a godsend, manna from heaven. Years later, I realized that he had casually encouraged me to undertake a monumental task. He suggested that I do *imagery therapy* with my father. When I asked him what that was, he told me about the Simonton method (Simonton & Simonton, 1981). The Simontons of California had developed the technique of having children with cancer talk to the disease, create mental images, and then draw them. The Simontons reported success with the procedure. I was desperate, vulnerable, and very dependent on Dr. K., and trusted him unreservedly. I decided to try anything that he suggested to help my father.

At first it actually worked. I would sit at his bedside in the hospital and he would talk to the disease, draw it, and I would listen. First pictures of ugly creatures and then drawings of children in a circle playing emerged. Amazingly, the doctors reported that the blood tests showed improvement. I was elated.

Then one day, not long thereafter, he told me that he didn't want to do the imagery therapy any more. Looking back, I think he was telling me that he was ready to die. I was shattered. But when I went back to the group to report the bad news, something equally horrible happened.

In front of the whole group, Dr. K. became defensive and turned on me when he said, "Well, no wonder your father wants to stop the imagery therapy. Look at how depressed you are!" I was too dumbfounded to even respond. It was as if he had stabbed me in the chest. I was terribly wounded and couldn't speak. It was as if he too had died for me that night. The group colluded with him, protecting him from close scrutiny. He tacitly supported their complicity by remaining silent as the group concurred. They agreed; who could blame my father for stopping the imagery therapy with me, as depressed as I was? Sitting there in a daze for the rest of that group, I felt like I was dying too. I left group that night even more depressed and anxious than I had been when I walked in. And the long tailspin began. First, like a loyal son, I protected Dr. K. I couldn't imagine losing both my fathers at the same time, so I took out my combined fury at him for having betrayed me, abandoning me in a time of desperate need, and the fury at myself, for having failed both my fathers, on myself.

Obviously, I lived to tell the story. And clearly, not all iatrogenic treatment reactions are as horrific as this one. But it is a cautionary tale. I trusted him implicitly, perhaps even too much. In retrospect, I see that it was naïve of me to do so. For his part, Dr. K.'s unwillingness or inability to take responsibility for having directed me on a quixotic quest was crazy-making. And yet I stayed with him for some years thereafter, until I was emotionally strong enough to leave.

Another goal of this book, therefore, is to show how the tremendous healing power of group may be jeopardized if the leader does not take responsibility for the consequences of having blurred the boundaries of treatment. While altered boundaries may be a fact of life in many group therapy milieus, it is not necessarily the case that damage will be done to members. In order to protect their emotional, and even physical well-being, leaders in altered frame environments need to be eternally vigilant to the possibility that not all negative treatment reactions are distortions, and further to be willing to openly address these instances both in the group and with colleagues in supervision.

For the moment, suffice it to say that the unfolding of these events seemed to have led inextricably toward writing an account of my experience training as a group leader, which in turn also led me to develop an eye for signs of iatrogenic treatment reactions in other patient/trainees in altered frame therapy relationships, some of whom I knew personally or of whom I had heard. And finally, I write because I have known people who weren't as fortunate as I have been and who have forever gotten lost to alcoholism and to mental collapse in part as a result of their inability to extricate themselves from the destructive entanglement of their dual relationships. It is for these reasons that I feel compelled to take on this project.

I should note from the outset that the examples, cases, and scenarios that are presented in this book are anecdotal in nature. They do not constitute an empirical survey of the state of the group therapy profession and therefore are not necessarily representative of the vast majority of clinicians. However, this book is an exposé of the abuses of power that can and do exist in the field. In some instances, the facts presented are based on my direct observation and, in others, colleagues who have shared these concerns have reported them to me.

As we shall see time and again throughout this work, even under the most ideal circumstances, most patients (except perhaps for borderlines) tend to protect the therapist from their negative assessments of the clinician's behavior and personality. They simply don't say everything, even when told to do so. While this reluctance to confront may be reflective of the patient's own neurotic character, at times it is not. At times it reflects an unconscious collusion between the parties—to blur the difference between reality and distortion. This is often a significant factor in distinguishing a successful analysis from one that is not.

This, then, is the theme of this book. Altering the frame of treatment always has consequences. I believe that is self-deluding, on the part of the leader, to believe that one is invulnerable from the costs of blurring the boundary between therapy and not-therapy simply by virtue of one's skill, clinical experience, and expertise. There are both clinical and ethical implications of practicing group treatment beyond the wisdom and knowledge of the profession. A moral dilemma exists when clinicians choose to do so.

This book is divided into six chapters. Chapter 1 addresses the importance of frame maintenance in group therapy, and answers the question of "Why group therapy?" I lay out my understanding of why group therapy has value, of the way group works, and of the healing power of analytic group therapy. I also make an argument for the necessity of a secure-frame treatment environment in order for that healing power to occur. Chapter 2 is devoted to a description of dual relationships between practicing group therapists at analytic training institutes, and their impact on patient/trainees is explored. Chapter 3 is devoted to a discussion of the social structure and character structure of clinicians who train at cult-like institutes. It details the intrapersonal, interpersonal, and organizational forces that sustain these relationships. Chapter 4 elucidates the inherent paradox of the role of group therapy member and the irrational emotions that often underlie treatment choices. In Chapter 5, I outline the seven dangers of blurred boundaries between therapy and not-therapy. Chapter 6 offers my findings from interviews with other group therapists about their experiences with blurred boundaries. This is a presentation of the untoward experiences of both group therapists in their own treatment and of laymen who have courageously chosen to talk about the conspiracy of silence. The Epilogue is a note on the duality of trust and betrayal in analytic group psychotherapy.

A resolution of the harmful effects of emotional incest in group psychotherapy lies within the social structure of the profession itself. The seeds of reform have already been planted. An authentic solution to what Philip Slater has called "inner circuitry thinking" is found through group process (Pepper, 1991).

Newton's First Law of Motion applies to the world of interpersonal relations as well as the physical one: "An object at rest tends to stay at rest unless acted upon by an outside force." Inertia can be countered by action. The insular and secretive nature of the conspiracy of silence is vulnerable to exposure. Open airing and discussion has the potential to ameliorate some of the damage of blurred boundaries in treatment. Those clinicians who have bravely come forward and shared with me their experiences, here in print and at workshops and open sessions at professional conferences, have added to the momentum in restructuring the way group leaders are trained and, as a result, the way group treatment is delivered to the general population of group patients. This is an encouraging sign for the future, and a positive step toward providing the highest quality service for the powerful and healing modality of group psychotherapy.

NOTE

1. See Joyce Slochower's (2014) *Psychoanalytic Collisions (2nd Edition)* for a discussion of similar phenomena in individual psychotherapy

Acknowledgments

This book about the incestuous nature of the interpersonal relationships at many group training institutes across this country is a story of human foibles within our healing profession, and the courage of those individuals who have chosen to face them. I am indebted to all of my therapists and teachers that have encouraged me to face mine. Rosalind Kaplan, Phd., and Gerald Appel M.S.W. stand out as having been important sources of strength, support, and wisdom.

Special thanks to my colleague and friend, Lee Kassan, M.A. for his expert editorial suggestions and his gentle yet effective way of guiding me through the book writing process. I am grateful to my wonderful fiancée, Lois Dorman, for her unwavering support of this project, enthusiasm, critical reading of the manuscript, and excellent suggestions. I am also fortunate to have had the encouragement and support of my brilliant daughter, Alison Pepper Atanasio, whose feedback was invaluable in moving the project forward. I would also like to thank my editor, Amy King, for her guidance in keeping my writing on point.

I am thankful to those colleagues and friends, like Helene Satz, who have allowed me to interview them and to use their experiences as vignettes in this work. Without their stories, this book could have not been written. They have been courageous in confronting the conspiracy of silence.

Chapter One

The Importance of the Frame and Why Group Therapy

A well-run therapy group *is* like a member's first group experience in that participants see others in the group as significant people in their lives and re-create these relationships in the group. A group that is structured as a secure frame, one in which members are anonymous to each other outside the group and the leader's relationship to the members is solely doctor to patient, allows the group therapist to be reasonably certain that his or her observations of the manner in which members re-create their families of origin in the group are accurate. This then allows the leader to understand the manner in which members undermine themselves in their adult relationships, revealing the member's unique character defenses and personality dynamics, in vivo. This is a method that is not readily accessible for an individual therapist to apprehend directly. That is the healing potential of group.

There are many books on analytic group therapy. This one is unique. It is both a presentation of the healing power of group and an exposé of the abuses of power that occur when leaders blur boundaries between therapy and not therapy, thereby altering the frame of treatment. For the purpose of this discussion, "the frame refers to the nature of the relationship between the therapist and the patient in which both relinquish a desire for a real relationship in favor of an 'as if' quality that then permits the relationship itself to be a focus of examination" (West & Livesley, 1986, p. 6).

One goal is to alert the professional community of group therapists to the often unseen dangers of altered frame group therapy. I believe this book would also be of interest to past, present, and future group therapy members and to anyone interested in reading an insider's look into largely overlooked, and potentially destructive, dynamics of this type of treatment modality. It specifically refers to analytic group therapy as opposed to other types, like supportive group therapy, cognitive-behavioral therapy, or dialectal group therapy. In analytic group treatment the nature of the relationships between the leader and members and between the members *is* the treatment.

This kind of treatment is sometimes referred to as *transference* group therapy because the assumption is that members will perceive and react to others in the group as they would perceive and react to significant others in their lives, thereby repeating the same dysfunctional interpersonal patterns from real life in these "as if" relationships in group. This is what gives group (throughout the book, I will use the word group to mean group therapy) its healing power but it works most effectively in a secure frame milieu. Langs (1989) addresses this issue in regard to the referral process for individual psychotherapy. To quote: "How you know your therapist—and what you know about him or her—becomes part of your therapy" (Langs, 1989, p.79). I have modified his point to fit group:

> *The manner in which group members know each other and what they know about each other, and the manner in which they know the group leader and what they know about him or her, all have a profound effect on the course of treatment and its outcome.*

Even the latest edition of Yalom's (2005) classic text, *The Theory and Practice of Group Psychotherapy*, does not include a discussion of frame alterations for outpatient group treatment. My premise is that the frame is a variable, and like any important variable it needs to be taken into account in the assessment of the helpfulness of group treatment. An examination of the extent to which the leader has built safeguards for frame maintenance must be included in any equation of group therapy's efficacy. To ignore its variability among the differing schools of thought within the analytic group treatment community constitutes a blind spot in the profession. It is in this way that my book differs from the rest. My supposition is that neglecting the frame obviates the prevailing assumption that boundaries are a given and renders it invalid.

My concept of *secure frame* is similar to that of Robert Langs (1977). Secure frame treatment means: 1) that the relationship between member and leader is exclusively professional and that they are only known to each other in their roles as leader and as group member (2004a, 2014a, p.56); 2) that the treatment takes place in a safe environment, such as a professional office building or in a home office that is separate from the leader's living quarters (Pepper, 2003b, Maroda, 2000, p.20-21); 3) that the leader abides by the ethical precept of informed consent, which means the fee is mutually agreed upon at the start of treatment and the prospective member is told that there will be periodic fee increases. Further, these increases are based on objective criteria such as inflation, increases in cost of living, and advances in the leader's training and experience rather than on subjective criteria like greed, the leader's sense of deprivation, or, worse, revenge (Pepper, 2003a, 2013, p.138).

There is a concept from chaos theory that seems apt here. That concept—"the sensitive dependence on initial conditions" (Gleick, 1986, p.8) also known as the Butterfly Effect—refers to the phenomena in nature where small changes in input at time one can produce large changes in output at time two. In other words, so the logic goes, if a butterfly flaps its wings over the Pacific Ocean, this slight change in wind current can reverberate through the atmosphere creating significant alterations in weather patterns days later on the West Coast of the US. Perhaps, this is a bit of an exaggeration of reality, but the point is well taken that we live in an ecological world where all things are connected. Alterations of the frame can lead to unplanned and to largely uncontrolled changes in the treatment that are not necessarily for the better.

My assumption is that no authentic intimacy is possible in group therapy, or in real life for that matter, without emotional separateness. Maintaining the frame of treatment is quite difficult at any level of training and experience, because of the natural tendency of both leaders and members to defend against the anxiety of separateness by blurring boundaries (Langs, 1982). Simply said, maintaining boundaries creates anxiety and blurring them temporarily decreases it. Leaders who blur boundaries, consciously or not, diminish their own anxiety and that of their groups, but they do so at a high cost.

They risk losing valuable leverage in interpreting all negative treatment reactions as transference and resistance (Fenichel, 1974). Sadly, it is the group members who must bear the brunt of this cost. As we shall see, blurred boundaries often lead to iatrogenic treatment reactions, reactions that are related to the treatment itself, symptoms such as depression and anxiety. Without a secure frame it is not possible to know for certain what the origins of the symptoms are.

Writers of varying theoretical orientations have largely overlooked the impact of alterations of the frame on group treatment. They take for granted that transference and resistance are the result of the group's and its members' distortions of reality, misrepresentations of the present that are based on historical artifacts. I contend that, without an understanding of the important role played by the frame of treatment, it is impossible for the group therapist as observer to discern reality from distortion. Without this clarity, harm may be done. While there is an element of transference in all group interactions, the valence is skewed away from transference and resistance when the frame is altered.

In order for the leader to objectively comprehend the group's and the individual members' unique reluctance to abide by the contract, which in group is to "say how you feel toward the other members and why you feel that way," it must be implicit that secure boundaries characterize the treatment environment. To say everything when boundaries are blurred is unwise at best, emotionally and even physically dangerous at worst. Under these conditions, saying everything is obviated by the treatment itself.

It is therefore the leader's obligation to provide such a safe environment for the process of group treatment to play out. Without such assurance, it is impossible to know whether the failure of the member to abide by the contract is a resistance or transferential, rather than it being iatrogenic, i.e., a realistic response to a contaminated environment; that is, whether the negative treatment reaction is related to the treatment itself rather than a reflection of members' distortions. The underlying assumption of psychoanalytically-oriented group therapy is that in order to distinguish objective from subjective negative reactions to the treatment, a clear frame of treatment must exist.

One unintended consequence of a secure-frame environment is that it has the power, if the leader allows it, to keep him emotionally honest. It is much more difficult for a leader to hide behind the role of therapist than it is for the individual therapist for at least two separate but related reasons: 1) there are witnesses. If only one member calls the leader out on some questionable behavior then it is possible that it is transference, or for it to be interpreted as such. I will have more to say about this phenomenon when I write about the 10 Percent Rule in psychotherapy. If the group sees it, however, then the leader had better believe that self-examination is in order. The entire group's perception cannot be wrong; and 2) the group setting allows for greater therapist transparency. Idiosyncratic behavior patterns are more readily identified. They stand out in high relief because the leader's relationship to group members is confined solely to that milieu. There is no seepage from outside the group social contact to contaminate the interactions.

For instance, when I added a new member to an ongoing group, he immediately proceeded to provoke the entire group. The newcomer was a very bright, arrogant, and contentious fellow whom I initially saw with his wife for a couple's consultation. She was ready to divorce him because of his controlling and tyrannical behavior. In fact, this fellow had come to the US from another country where he held high positions in both the university and the government. He had so alienated the leader of his own country that he was told to leave or suffer the consequences. I thought that this man needed group. He had no idea how he came across in relationships. He actually thought that he was helping people, when in fact he was putting them off.

That first night in group, he went around the room analyzing each member's neurosis, telling them what was wrong with their personalities and making suggestions as to how they could improve their lives. His unsolicited advice was unwanted and self-serving. He was hiding a great sense of inadequacy through his air of superiority; and the group hated him for it. I told him that it would be best that he just listen before he was asked to leave *this* group, as a parallel to his past experience.

As a newcomer he had not earned the privilege of confronting members on their foibles. That would only come when he had developed relationships with them that included his revealing his own vulnerabilities before pointing out the weaknesses of others. He stayed a total of two sessions before quitting the group. After he exited, one group member, John, lambasted me for having brought this "pompous ass" into the group. He demanded that I justify my decision.

My knee-jerk reaction was to become defensive and deflect it back onto them. "Why do you think I brought him in?" I asked. But the group wouldn't have it. I realized that a revolt was at hand. I knew that this was a time to answer honestly. "Look. I knew this guy would be a tough nut to crack: I didn't think he would stay very long in group. But I'm egotistical enough to think that I could have held on to this guy. I made myself a bet that I could get him to stay in group for at least eight sessions. Obviously, I lost the bet."

The point of this story is that the secure frame provided structure for me as well as the members. The situation called for authenticity. I could not readily hide behind the role of leader and turn the focus back onto the group. I took responsibility for my decision, which took pressure off the group and allowed us to move on.

The theme of this book is: alterations of the frame always have consequences for the treatment. Further that without secure boundaries, group therapy may be compromised. It is my belief that when boundaries are blurred, as is the case of such frame alterations as dual relationships, running groups from the home office, and raising fees for other than objective reasons, then negative treatment reactions may occur that are iatrogenic in origin and are therefore not purely transference.

Physicists tell us that to understand a phenomenon is to know its boundaries. To know where one entity ends, and another begins, is an essential component of living in harmony with the environment. At the same time, the maintenance of boundaries produces a tension in all living organisms. There seems to be a natural urge to surrender boundaries and merge with the universe. Initially exhilarating, this experience also can become catastrophic. Such is the case in psychoanalytic group psychotherapy when boundaries are blurred between members and the leader and between members themselves in a variety of social contexts.

At best the treatment is diluted; at worst it is contaminated. This book elucidates the conditions under which the integrity of group treatment has been breached. In this way, the practitioner, unwittingly or not, may have violated the basic code of all healing professions, the Hippocratic Oath, which states: "Above all else, do no harm." In a blurred boundary environment the interpretation of all group members' negative treatment reactions as transference or resistance may be crazy-making. Reality can get turned on its head, and a "mad-hatter's tea party"–like world may prevail. R. D. Laing (1970) once said that the fastest way to drive someone mad is to invalidate his or her perception of reality.

WHY GROUP THERAPY?

Over the last 70 years, the field of group psychotherapy has emerged from its roots as an auxiliary to, and a less respected modality than, individual psychotherapy. When I'm asked why anyone would need group therapy, I reply, "Group therapy is for people who have problems with relationships." There are very few people on this earth who have never encountered any difficulties with others in either their personal or professional life or both. In fact, group is now the treatment of choice for many psychological conditions, particularly the treatment of patients with relationship difficulties, which, to my mind, covers just about everyone. Group can help in several ways (Yalom & Leszcz, 2005). For example, many people simply cannot see how they come across in relationships without the necessary feedback that a modality like group provides.

For example, a young man came to see me for a therapy consultation at the insistence of his girlfriend, who threatened to leave him if he didn't. When I suggested group treatment to help him with his relationship issues, he flatly refused. When asked why not he replied: "Because I'm not interested in other people's problems!" To which I responded: "Exactly! That is your problem."

As the reader may have surmised, I believe that most people can profit from a group therapy experience. Despite my own experience, I consider the healing power of group, in the right hands, to be substantial. In fact, it is my conviction that an individual psychotherapy patient's treatment is not complete without some time spent in group therapy. But timing is everything. Not everyone is ready for group at the beginning of their therapy experience. Most people need to spend some time in individual treatment prior to entering a group, because people who seek out individual therapy seek attention. People who seek out group therapy seek relationships.

Usually, an individual requires some time alone with a therapist before they are emotionally ready for the often "rough and tumble" of group interaction. Prospective group members need time to explore, in private, their personal stumbling blocks to intimacy and to develop the thick skin that is necessary to tolerate and to use constructive, but sometimes painful, group feedback. These stumbling blocks are related to the fear of intimacy.

Ormont (1974) has identified four basic fears that interfere with the establishment of healthy interpersonal relationships: 1) fear of engulfment, such as the group isolate who doesn't participate in group interactions lest he be contaminated by the emotions of others; 2) fear of vulnerability, such as the young man in group who speaks very little about the emotionally intimate details of his life for fear that the others will find him wanting and unworthy of their love and attention; 3) fear of loss of impulse control, such as the repressed woman in group who fears that even talking about sex will propel her into action; and 4) fear of abandonment, such as the man who keeps himself aloof in group because he knows that to have someone is to lose someone.

Some prospective group members are quite hesitant to begin treatment for these reasons. They are convinced that the group experience will be like their original group experience, that is, like their family of origin. And who wants to repeat that? But they actually may be right but for the wrong reason.

For example, a female borderline patient in individual therapy with me complained bitterly about the mistreatment she suffered at the hands of her sisters. She presented herself as a helpless victim of her sisters' meanness. I suspected that her insistence on being seen as a victim was her defense against feeling guilty, but about what I did not know. After a year of individual treatment in which I attempted to help this woman to understand her need to be the victim, but to no avail, I invited her to join a treatment group. The woman was leery of group. She couldn't see how group would help, but she trusted my judgment enough to give it a try. She agreed to test it out.

But during her first meeting, she verbally assaulted all the women in the group, sarcastically finding fault with everything from their personalities to their choices of attire. I had to caution her to stop lest she be expelled from group after the initial session. In this one session, the patient unwittingly revealed a side of her that did not appear in a year's worth of individual treatment. This gave me valuable leverage in helping the patient take back some control of her family relationships by understanding her role in her own sense of victimization. She saw herself as a Cinderella who had to contend with wicked stepsisters. The extent to which this was actually the case in her family of origin was not relevant here. What was relevant was the way she saw it and so for her that was the reality.

However, in not having known the women in the group prior to her entry, I could reasonably assume that her perception in this case was skewed. In the individual treatment, she had my attention alone. In group she had to share it. Group therapy is inherently frustrating for this reason. The reality of the situation infuriated her but it also reminded her of the sibling rivalry that did exist in her family growing up. While her rage was real, the emotion did not fit the current reality. It was a relic from the past. She imposed her old feelings onto the new group experience, hence the transference.

This was not something that she had conscious control of, although to her it felt like it was happening all over again. In her real family she sensed that she was not her parents' favorite. In treatment she wanted to kill off her group rivals with her words. It took her several months to be able to put these feelings into words and say that she felt jealous, rather than act out that feeling in the group.

As noted, the group leader's task is to observe members' behavior and to understand in vivo, rather than through storytelling, as is the case in individual psychotherapy, just how their fears of intimacy play out in the group. The leader can thus infer how these mechanisms operate in the members' lives outside of the group. In order to accomplish this, the leader must first establish a contract with the members. The basic contract of analytic group psychotherapy is this: members are to put their thoughts and feelings toward each other, and why they feel that way, into words.

The group leader expects, however, that sooner or later (usually sooner), the members will default on their agreement to comply with this contract. However, this is exactly what the leader wants to happen. In fact, it has to happen in order for the treatment to work. Defaulting on the contract opens the window to understanding the members' pattern of relating outside the group.

It is then the leader's responsibility to study and to analyze the group's and its members' resistance to saying everything. However, most practitioners of analytic group psychotherapy stop there and assume that, all things being equal, this is their major task in understanding the group. It is at this point that my understanding of group dynamics diverges from the work of many other group leaders.

Group therapists usually take as a given that negative treatment reactions are mostly transference and resistance, although this may not be the case. This is an assumption; it is not a fact. This assumption is so common in the field that it has a name. It is informally referred to in the profession as the 10 Percent Rule. The rule states that only 10 percent of patients' negative perceptions of the leader are in fact accurate. That is, a small proportion of the time, group members' negative perceptions of the leader are a precise assessment of the leader's character flaws and not a distortion of reality as transference would imply.

For example, in the case cited earlier of the woman who verbally attacked other women in the group during her first group session, part of the potential healing power of that experience was that the members were anonymous to each other. This anonymity allowed me to be reasonably assured that her negative reactions were part of her family-based transference. When members do have social contact, then negative treatment reactions cannot be so easily classified, as the following instance demonstrates.

In a training group of professional leaders who were affiliated with the same institute, a member complained that some members were part of the group therapist's inner circle. The group leader was also the administrator of the institute and as such had great power to award favored trainees with the benefits of the system in return for their loyalty to him. The complaining member, while a recipient of some these perks, like teaching and supervisory positions within the organization, was not in line for plumb perks like patient referrals and opportunities to represent the organization at conferences here and abroad. The members of the group labeled her complaints as grousing and reminded her of the sibling rivalry that existed in her family of origin and gave instances where she reported to the group that her father favored other siblings in her family. In other words, the group "gaslighted" her (Pepper, 2014a).

The term *gaslight* comes from the title of the classic movie of the 1940s. In the film the husband (Charles Boyer) attempts to drive his wife (Ingrid Bergman) mad by invalidating her perception of reality. In Chapter 5, more will be said about gaslighting.

Reminding her of her past undermined her perception of the present. The unspoken message was that her view of the current reality was distorted. But was it really a distortion? If in fact there were others who were favored over her, then her perception was more than just transference. In other words, the group invalidated her view of reality. This is crazy-making. The woman left the meeting feeling anxious and depressed. This was an iatrogenic treatment reaction, a reaction produced by the treatment itself.

This instance is very different from the one presented first. It is different because, in an environment where group members have social contact, the possibility that the transference is contaminated is quite high, unlike the first case, where members were anonymous to each other. In the second case, where group members were in fact treated differently in their interactions with the leader outside the group, it is not so clear to what the member was responding. Was it her own history of sibling rivalry that motivated her negative reaction or was there actually an in group that curried favor from the leader?

The group leader's unwillingness or inability to acknowledge the untenable position that this woman was in, by virtue of her dual relationships with him and with her fellow group members, constitutes more than an error in judgment. It tacitly condones the development of an iatrogenic treatment reaction, and as such is an abuse of power. That this type of substandard treatment may be endemic to the field is reflected in the following example. There seems to be a collective blind spot among group practitioners.

At a meeting of a peer supervision group of which I had been a member, a participant presented the case of a difficult patient in the treatment group that he ran. The member, a middle-aged woman, had become sullen and withdrawn in her interactions in the group. When the leader questioned her about her behavior, she cryptically replied that the group was not the place to talk about it. Instead of investigating with her what she meant by that, he interpreted her behavior. Acting out his exasperation with her apparently obstinate behavior, the leader reminded her of her last experience in another therapy group where she was asked to leave because of her unwillingness to cooperate with the treatment. In other words, he analyzed her in the service of his aggression toward her. It seemed to me that he acted out his countertransferential feelings toward her. It was no wonder she didn't feel safe enough to say what was on her mind.

During his presentation to the peer group, a fellow member said that she recognized the identity of this woman from the presenter's description of her. The fellow peer group member said that she, herself, had supervised this woman at the group training institute where the presenter was co-director. In other words, in addition to being his group patient, she was also his subordinate at the training institute.

I was surprised that this fact was not brought to the peer group's attention from the start. Apparently, the presenter did not consider it to be an important variable in understanding the case. Ironically, I had told the group at the beginning of this meeting that I was writing a book about altered-frame group therapy. I asked participants if any one of them had experience either as a member or a leader of a group in which members had complicated dual relationships. Everyone, including this presenter, said no.

In light of their complicated relationship, it was understandable why she didn't feel safe to talk in the group. In fact, her suspicions were confirmed by his interpretation of her behavior, which could be seen as a veiled attack. When I raised the question of whether this woman's reluctance to speak in group was perhaps in part related to the compromised position in that she was in both as the patient and as student of the leader, my concerns were roundly dismissed by the peer group. They were convinced that her negative treatment reaction was purely transference. When I asked, "How can you be sure it was transference, given the dual relationship that she was in with the leader?" the discussion was shut down with the unanimous response, "No, it's definitely transference. This woman has a history of failed relationships." While this may be the case, it seemed to me that it was not necessarily the only variable operating here.

This woman was in an impossible position. As a patient she was expected to say everything; as a student she was expected to be politic and withhold her most irrational thoughts and feelings lest she expose herself to negative evaluations by her superiors. She was in a double bind. The concept of the double bind was first developed by Gregory Bateson and colleagues (1956) in the classic article "Toward a Theory of Schizophrenia." It was his argument that schizophrenia is caused by the simultaneous and contradictory messages of an emotionally disturbed family environment. The identified patient can't respond to one message without clashing with the other conflicting one.

Since that peer group meeting, I have worried about this poor woman and wondered how she fared in the contaminated treatment environment where her perception of reality wasn't taken seriously. I wondered if she had developed iatrogenic symptoms of anxiety and depression. I never found out the deposition of this case because I took a leave of absence from the group after that session in order to devote time to write this book.

Sadly, this is not an isolated incident. The double bind of dual relationships will be a recurrent theme throughout this book. In the context of a group therapy experience, a double bind constitutes another instance of an abuse of power.

The next chapter is devoted to an examination of the clinical and ethical implications of these complicated relationships. It includes examples of similar instances where patient/trainees are in impossible predicaments that threaten their emotional stability, and some cases even their physical well-being.

While the main focus of this book is the impact of blurred boundaries between therapy and not therapy on the leaders' own group treatment, it is not the exclusive focus. The effect of the leaders' training on the larger population of group members is also a major concern. The manner in which leaders are trained is one of the most important determinants of the quality of care. Training in a boundary-less environment may be problematic with costs not only for neophyte leaders but for the group members that they treat in their practices (Pepper 2014a, p.56).

The leaders' own treatment and supervisory experience serve as a template for the development of their role as professional group therapists. Leaders trained in blurred boundary settings have told me that it feels "natural" for them to do it that way; and they can't imagine running groups in any other manner. A compromised frame of treatment has become part of the normative culture of their professional life. But despite their insular thinking, this is *not* the only way to conduct groups.

I call this process the "pass along effect" and it plays an important part in the delivery and the outcome of services to all members, be they professional group leaders themselves or not. Included in the following chapters, therefore, are also examples of the untoward group therapy experiences of some group members that are laymen, harmed when their leader's own compromised treatment experiences have been passed on to them.

However, there are some group leaders, trained in compromised treatment milieus, myself included, who have witnessed the potential dangers first-hand, and have decided to do it differently, making safety a priority by the creation of a secure frame treatment environment. The irony of all this is that the group therapy of group leaders may be the most compromised treatment of all (Pepper, 2014, p.55).

Chapter Two

Dual Relationships in Group Psychotherapy

The Pros & Cons

THE CONS FOR PATIENT/TRAINEES AT GROUP PSYCHOANALYTIC TRAINING INSTITUTES

I finally left the clinic and severed ties with my group therapist/supervisor/colleague/buddy. When I had gotten enough emotional distance from the whole experience, I began to search the literature for evidence of other therapists' exposure to complicated dual relationships at group analytic training institutes. I wanted to know if there was any substantiation that perhaps my experience with dual relationships was not unique in the profession. As luck would have it, I didn't have to look very far.

I recalled that many years prior, a former undergraduate sociology professor and mentor of mine at Queens College of CUNY, Dr. Joan Dulchin, had told me that her doctoral dissertation was about the lack of confidentiality at a psychoanalytic training institute. At that time, the topic didn't mean very much to me. I knew nothing about therapy, let alone analytic training institutes. I contacted Joan and she sent me a copy of an article that was a spinoff of her dissertation. That article, "The Ambiguity of Confidentiality at a Psychoanalytic Institute" (Dulchin & Siegal, 1982), fascinated me.

Although it described interactions at a training institute for individual psychoanalysis, there were similarities to my own experience in group training. I was intrigued by her depiction of the conflict of interest between teaching and treatment, and how the organization attempted to resolve that conflict, and, as Gans (1992) has noted in another context, interactions in group therapy take place in a more intense and complicated field than in individual therapy.

The contradictory expectations of the trainees at the training institute, explained in Dulchin's article are significant. She noted that, on the one hand, as a patient, an analytic candidate in individual psychotherapy training, is expected to say everything, but as a student, is expected to be politic and withhold irrational thoughts and feelings. Kassan (2010) noted that one reason for supervisees' nondisclosure of information in supervision is fear of "political suicide" (p. 35). Hence, the candidate's dilemma of dual relationships existed at analytic training institutes for individual psychotherapy.

I had reached the same conclusion she did for group training: No one really cared how the student felt. Actually, it was quite the opposite. The expression of thoughts and feelings criticizing the organization or its faculty could have damaging real-life consequences for the patient/trainee. The truth was that behavior was all that mattered. It was then that I had an "aha" moment. I made a connection between two apparently separate theories that I was already familiar with, but hadn't thought of as related until then.

I had read the work of Gregory Bateson and Jay Haley (1956) and their theory of the double bind, the article as referenced in Chapter 1. Bateson, Haley, Weakland, and Jackson (1956) had published a paper on their view of the etiology of schizophrenia. Their thesis was much like that of R. D. Laing (1970), who wrote that schizophrenia is a sane response to a crazy environment.

Bateson and his colleagues studied interactions of hospitalized female schizophrenics with their families, and found that episodes of psychotic behavior often followed incidents where the patient was given contradictory nonverbal messages from her parents. "Damned if you do and damned if you don't" was the phrase that summarized her dilemma (Bateson, 1956, p. 251). This seemed to me to parallel the dynamic in dual relationships at training institutes. At best, it would be unwise to say everything in group despite the directive to do so.

West and Livesley (1986) make the point that in analytic group therapy, where the goal is to foster character change, it is imperative that leaders "establish a frame explicitly and implicitly laying down a set of ground rules that define the conditions of relatedness between patients and themselves. Hence, therapists have to deprive themselves of the privilege of real relationships with their patients and concentrate instead on the task of establishing therapeutic relationships" (West & Livesley, 1986, p. 7). It seemed to me that narcissistic gratification served as one factor in the establishment of dual relationships at group training institutes, with potentially greater risk than at analytic individual training institutes.

For unlike training in individual psychoanalysis, in group training the bind is more than just inhibiting irrational thoughts and feelings lest the trainee be judged harshly by his or her superiors. Since group training obviously takes place in groups, where trainees may be simultaneously in supervision groups with their own group therapists and with fellow group members from their leader's treatment group, and thereby witness to a myriad of interactions between people in, around, and outside the institute, they would also be privy to aspects of their superiors' personalities and character structures, and further be privy to the playing out of the character dynamics of fellow group members as they interact with each other that would be inaccessible to them otherwise, hence the importance of maintaining the frame of treatment.

Potentially, they would be exposed to behavior that might be unflattering to their associates, or even worse. Some of these interactions could provide glimpses of others that might call into question their integrity and even their emotional stability. The question is with whom in the organization could the trainees freely share all their feelings and thoughts about the leaders' and fellow group members' inadvertent transparency without there being potential negative repercussions? To answer my own rhetorical question—no one.

In multiple-role relationships between practicing group therapists (the terms *multiple role* and *dual relationships* are used interchangeably), senior group leaders are involved with their patients in a variety of extra-treatment roles such as supervisor, colleague, teacher, administrator, friend, and even relative. In other words, as Raubolt (2006) notes, these relationships are both professional and personal. In this context, *socially involved* refers to any role relationship in addition to a clean, fee-for-service doctor—patient connection. These relationships are distinguished from the inevitable social interactions that can occur between group leaders and their patients who are also practicing group therapists. Crossing paths at professional conferences and socializing at organization events are unavoidable. Although these events have meaning and engender feelings for all participants, they are incidental to the treatment and therefore are not of the same order of experience as multiple-role relationships. Further, patient/trainees have complicated and competitive relationships with each other. In addition to being fellow patients of the same group leader, they can be fellow supervisees, students, colleagues, friends, and relatives (Pepper, 2002).

It is my conviction that any therapist who engages in dual relationships, and who simultaneously accepts the existence of the unconscious, would be wise to consider the possibility that these relationships blur the boundaries of treatment. And that in blurring the boundaries, there is always a potential for danger that is unseen. This constitutes a violation of the basic ethical code of all healing professions—the Hippocratic Oath, which states: "Above all else, do no harm." It is for this reason that several professional organizations have deemed dual relationships to be unethical (American Psychological Association, 2002; Federation of Clinical Social Workers, 1997).[1] . The APA Code of Ethics states that psychologists should “make every effort to avoid dual relationships with clients and/or increase the risk of client exploitation” (p.4). Dual relationships are also unethical because they violate confidentiality.

Further, my observations have shown that the role of group therapist itself, coupled with the clinician’s dominant personality, can insulate the practitioner from the anxiety associated with the fluidity of blurred boundaries that are directly related to dual relationships. Sadly, it is often the patient who must bear the consequences of blurred boundaries (Pepper, 1997). If patients are held responsible for most treatment resistances under these conditions, then a clinical and ethical problem may exist (Temerlin & Temerlin, 1982). There is a possibility that a negative treatment reaction may be iatrogenic, but not interpreted as such.

Within the community of group training institutes, it is not uncommon for senior therapists to be socially involved with their patients, and for the patients to be involved with each other. The social structure of some group training institutes is defined largely by these relationships. As Raubolt (2006) notes, not all affiliations to institutes or training groups are destructive.

For example, he refers to the research of Harwood (1998), who wrote that in institutes where dual relationships are prohibited, for example, there is an opportunity for “connectedness, affiliation, attachment and security” (quoted in Raubolt, 2006, p. 175). There is a continuum of types of group training experiences that are largely based on the existence of dual relationships. This reality is made painfully clear in Annette Richard’s (2006) harrowing account of her dual relationship experience in the psychotherapy cult CFT (Center for Feeling Therapy), where abusive leaders drove her to the brink of madness. She was without anyone within the organization who could provide a reality check. The fact that she voluntarily participated in her own subjugation is an important factor in understanding the power of cult-like training institutes.[2]

Although she entered this institute of her own free will, and not under duress, she behaved passively once inside the organization. Her inability and/or her unwillingness to say everything, thereby keeping too much to herself, all contributed to her becoming emotionally unstable.

Bazilian (1993) refers to this type of phenomenon in individual therapy as *diatrogenic*, as it derives from the dyad. Perhaps in group therapy it should be called *griatrogenic* (which would be a mouthful). In any case, it is a condition specifically brought about by the group therapist’s need to control and manipulate, stemming from unresolved grandiosity and omnipotence (Bazilian, 1993, p. 158).

What happened to Annette Richard constituted an abuse of power on the part of her superiors at the institute. That she didn’t talk to anyone about her experience while at the institute is a clear example of the patient/trainee’s dilemma. It is an instance of a conspiracy of silence that appears to characterize the social structure of many training institutes.

An article by Jane and Maurice Temerlin (1982) entitled "Psychotherapy Cults: An Iatrogenic Perversion of Treatment," pointed to a confluence of factors that produced negative treatment reactions as a result of dual relationships. Since not all trainees who engaged in them had suffered ego dysfunction, personality and character structure had to play some role in their development. Dual relationships alone could account for only a portion of an explanation of the problem. There had to be other factors as well.

The Temerlins wrote about five group psychotherapy training institutes in the Midwest. While unpublished and unknown outside their circle, the leaders ran their institutes like religious cults. According to the Temerlins, the similarities were: 1) the leaders were charismatic, brilliant, authoritarian, narcissistic, grandiose, and paranoid; 2) group members idealized the leader. The positive transference was accepted as reality, negative transference was interpreted as distortion; 3) a groupthink environment existed, contemptuous of other schools of thought. The leaders' theories were accepted at face value without empirical support. Critical thinking was discouraged; 4) members isolated themselves from others, including their own families. This was the norm; 5) followers joined by becoming patients of the leader during times of transition in their lives when security needs were greatest; 6) members organized their lives around the leader; 7) groups were cohesive. Members considered themselves to be part of an elite collection of professionals (Temerlin & Temerlin, 1982, p. 135). I would add an additional similarity: 8) leaders used intimidation and brainwashing tactics to frighten skeptical members who talked about leaving the cult-like training institutes. On more than one occasion, I have witnessed charismatic leaders tell members who were considering leaving the fold that their lives would fall apart if they did so. Iatrogenic treatment reactions are not limited to institutes run like religious cults by charismatic leaders, published or not. They exist wherever dual relationships exist.

The allure of these relationships can be quite formidable. The perceived benefits of such complicated relationships are high; otherwise, how professionals, who should know better, could be willing to compromise their treatment seems unfathomable. Later in this chapter, two questions are addressed that I would imagine the reader is asking: first, how do analytically oriented group therapists justify their decision to bend the rules of treatment given the knowledge of the dangers of blurred boundaries? And second, what is the motivation of those patient/therapists who seek out and remain in treatment with senior group leaders even after the onset of iatrogenic treatment reactions?

According to the Temerlins, some apparently bright and perceptive student/trainees decompensated after years of progress and growth in treatment once they entered a dual relationship with the leader. After years of a strong, positive, professional, clean, fee-for-service relationship with the leader, treatment progress ceased. Treatment among some of these patient/therapists reached intractable impasses. In extreme cases, the ego dysfunction deteriorated to suicidal proportions. The Temerlins believe the decompensation was a result of these patient/trainees knowing too much about their group leader's darker side. The overlapping of boundaries provided these people with a view of the leader that was neither flattering nor accessible to others.

Coupled with the social structure of the organization that fostered the development of an unspoken rule of silence, much like the Mafia's code of *omerta*, an open airing of these perceptions was precluded. In much the same way as in Annette Richard's experience, patient/trainees were driven crazy when their attempts to share their negative perceptions were invalidated by an unconscious collusion between the leaders and other members.

There was complicity in protecting the leader from too close scrutiny. I have labelled these phenomena The Emperor's New Clothes effect, and will explain it in greater detail in Chapter 5, which is devoted to a presentation of the seven dangers of blurred boundaries.

The Temerlins saw the development of symptoms as a direct consequence of this invalidating process. Their work gave further validity to my thought that dual relationships produce iatrogenic treatment reactions. The depictions of the social and emotional environment of these organizations are consistent with my observations. The Temerlins uncannily describe the characteristics of ego dysfunction that were associated with these complicated multiple-role relationships. The symptoms of the therapist/trainees that they described mirrored my own. They were:

1. The presence of ego decompensation. Depending on the nature of the extra-treatment contact, the iatrogenesis can range from the mild discomfort of role confusion, where it is not clear whether the group therapist is the patient/trainee's doctor or buddy, to destabilizing anxiety and depression, where the symptoms resemble a narcissistic transference, such as self-loathing, suicidal ideation, fantasies of self-mutilation, high levels of anxiety coupled with agitation, or extreme discomfort about the body. Patients report feeling that they are "falling apart" or "jumping out of their skin."

In the former instance, for example, when I joined the group leader's training institute, I found out that one of my fellow group members, also a therapist at the clinic, was a regular player in our group therapist's weekly poker game. "The Case of Sonny," to be presented shortly, illustrates a very serious destabilizing effect of dual relationships. Temerlin and Temerlin (1982) report that some patient/trainees who are socially involved with their group therapists have experienced ego decompensation to the point of suicide, when their realistic negative perceptions of the leader gleaned from contact outside the treatment were invalidated in their treatment groups. Other members sheltered the leader from close scrutiny and the patient/trainee was scapegoated, another one of the seven dangers of blurred boundaries that are described in Chapter 5. In a form of twisted loyalty, scapegoated patient/trainees often jettisoned their own view of reality, accepted the group's version, and then quite literally attacked themselves. Just like the Temerlins' subjects, I too had suffered from high levels of anxiety and depression as a result of the blurring of boundaries of treatment and supervision.

2. The dysfunction occurs well into the treatment after the establishment of a "normal" transference process. As in my case, in which the symptoms appeared years into the treatment, after engaging in imagery therapy with my father and his subsequent death, the onset of symptoms occurred *after* entering a dual relationship with the group leader.

3. Symptoms abate after disengaging from the institute and dual relationships. After severing ties and leaving the institute and the clinic with which it was affiliated, I recovered. That is, symptoms generally abate *after the patient/trainee terminates treatment, and severs all contact with the senior group therapist.*

It was reaffirming to learn that the Temerlins had observed a distinct pattern to the effects of these boundary-less relationships for some patient/trainees. To some extent, this pattern transcended their idiosyncratic character dynamics and the social structure of these organizations played a part as well.

In succeeding individual treatment, my therapist, Dr. Roz Kaplan, attempted to relieve my sense of guilt about having participated in such a destructive process by insisting that I wasn't responsible for what happened. She said that because of my age at the time (late twenties), I didn't know any better. She said that I had been psychologically naïve; but I agreed with the Temerlins. They argued that such an approach kept the patient/therapist from having to fully accept his role as a willing participant, with its attendant secondary-gain gratification, in his own subjugation. To deny the victim's full participation is to deny him the opportunity to take responsibility for his part in it.

Inspired to write about a configuration that now seemed to me to be more than just personal, I began to see the same pattern over and again in others as well. But it would not be until several years after the publication of my first article that I began to receive feedback from my peers that I was on the right track.

When I presented the results of my findings, from my first paper, at a poster session at the annual meeting of the American Group Psychotherapy Association in Washington, D.C., in 1994, conference attendees took notice. On a large board, I displayed an outline of the general features of the hazards of multiple-role relations, the personality traits of group leaders who participated in them, and the iatrogenic effects of these relationships on patient/

trainees. And although I mentioned no one by name, attendees from all over the country approached me and said that the description resembled institutes of various theoretical orientations (such as gestalt, psychoanalytic, modern analytic, self-psychological) and the individuals who populated them, from the West Coast to the East Coast and cities in between.

This pervasiveness seemed to suggest that the establishment of multiple-role relations transcended the character structure of leaders, as well as the variations in their theoretical orientations. I reasoned that, at least in part, the problem might be systemic and inherent to the structure of these organizations. The Temerlins noted that iatrogenic treatment reactions could occur at any training institute where dual relationships exist, independently of whether those organizations were cult-like in structure. As shall be discussed below, my own research supported this.

The feedback and encouragement of my peers were a motivation to add force to the reliability of the Temerlins' observations. What follows is a culling of my initial analysis, the Temerlins' study, and the observations of others on the incidence of ego dysfunction among analytic group trainees at institutes where dual relationships exist. It was to take more than twenty years for me to finally put all the pieces of the puzzle together.

Before moving to the next section, I would like to present the reader with an example of the type of ego dysfunction that I am referring to. When I originally published this vignette, I wrote without revealing that I was present in the room when it took place. Now I write as a participant—observer. And although it occurred almost thirty years ago, my memory of it is still quite vivid.

The Case of Sonny

I was a member of a training group run by a famous and charismatic leader. Sonny, a longtime group member and a seasoned group therapist, who had been in a complicated multiple-role relationship with this leader, told us that he had begun to experience symptoms of ego decompensation. An explanation of how and why I joined another group, with the same type of leader as my original one, appears in the epilogue.

Sonny told the leader, in front of the group, that he "felt psychotic, like my body is floating out of the chair." Not only was he anxious, but he was extremely depressed as well. He said that he thought of himself as an "ass kisser," someone who had to ingratiate himself to others in order to be liked. His story had a ring of déjà vu. What had happened to me was happening again, but this time to someone else; and it was unfolding right before my eyes.

The leader interpreted these symptoms as a narcissistic transference reaction, related to Sonny's conflicted relationship with his own father. I knew that this interpretation, while it may have had some measure of truth, wasn't the whole story, and in fact it was self-serving and abusive to Sonny. It drew attention away from the leader's responsibility for having created this compromised treatment relationship with him, and by labelling it as transference, i.e., a distortion, tacitly blamed the victim for it. This was an example of "gaslighting." I thought, *What a coward the leader is for doing this to Sonny.* I *knew* that Sonny's reaction could not only be a distortion of reality. Here's why.

It was common knowledge in the group that not only was Sonny the leader's patient and supervisee, but he was also his administrative assistant, confidante, and chauffeur. I believed that Sonny's symptoms were iatrogenic because of this multiple-role relationship. While I knew that Sonny was close to the leader, I also knew that he wasn't in the leader's inner circle. I imagined that Sonny was quite angry about his emasculated position in the organization, yet was unwilling to jeopardize his special closeness to the leader. In an act of twisted loyalty, Sonny protected the leader at his own emotional expense, just as I did in my own group therapy, and then he verbally attacked himself.

I had the impulse to say something, but to whom and about what? I knew that if I accused the leader of "gaslighting" poor Sonny, I ran the risk of engendering the group's wrath and becoming a scapegoat myself. I didn't trust the leader to protect me by owning up to his part in this. I believed that if I confronted him in the group my words would be dismissed. I turned to Sonny, who was sitting right next to me in the group circle, and said softly, simply, and obliquely, "This is not all your problem."

I didn't think he knew what I was talking about because he took the leader's lead and went on to talk about his relationship with his father. It was at this point that I knew that Sonny was a goner. He had abdicated his perception of reality in order not to jeopardize the leader's approbation. If Sonny were really interested in what I had to say, he would contact me later, after the group. He never did. But I was satisfied for having said something to him. I had broken the conspiracy of silence this time.

But there was another problem for Sonny. In not having learned about appropriate boundaries in his own treatment, he passed the problem along to patients in his own practice. For example, he used a patient's personal relationship with a jeweler to buy himself a precious stone.

An important assumption that underlies the premise of this book is that the manner in which group leaders are trained has consequences for the way in which they practice their craft. In Chapter 5, I describe these phenomena. I have called this process the *pass-along effect*, another of the seven dangers, because it has repercussions for the general population of group members in treatment with institute-trained leaders.

Review of the Literature

As noted in Chapter 1, when I read the description of the concept of "sensitive dependency on initial conditions" (Gleick, 1986, p.8), also known as the Butterfly Effect, my thoughts coalesced and I began to see the whole picture. Dual relationships were just one facet of a more general issue of alterations of the frame of group treatment; and that all frame changes had consequences for the treatment, even if they did not rise to the level of boundary violations.

Over the years, I would come to view such diverse phenomena as dual relationships, running groups from the home office, and raising group fees as frame alterations. Further, while I agreed with the Temerlins that the dual relationships could produce iatrogenic treatment reactions, the process by which this occurred was not entirely clear. I now believe that the negative effects of dual relationships are the last part of an eight-step process.

These factors are: 1) the narcissistic character structure and personality of the leaders, who view patient/trainees as objects, which leads to 2) the decision to blur the boundaries between treatment and not-treatment through the establishment of dual relationships; 3) lacking empathy, the leader puts his or her needs before the group's, thereby sacrificing the members' need for the emotional safety of a secure frame environment, which 4) allows for the valuation of gratification above analysis for leaders and group members alike, which 5) creates a collective blind spot that obscures thinking through the consequences of altering the frame of treatment; 6) a willingness on the part of patient/trainees to comply with this compromised treatment arrangement and the need to duplicate the transference in the treatment, i.e., to morph the transference into reality; 7) the institutionalization of a social structure at training organizations that adopts, supports, and maintains the conditions under which iatrogenic treatment reactions can occur, and 8) the development of a conspiracy of silence within the organization (see Chapter 4).

At the time that "When Transference Isn't Transference" was published (Pepper, 1990), except for the Temerlins' article (Temerlin & Temerlin, 1982) there had been very little written about dual relationships in group psychotherapy. This suggested to me that group therapists did not connect the blurring of boundaries through multiple-role relationships with iatrogenic conditions. It seemed that when a patient/trainee decompensated during the course of treatment, the decompensation was mostly viewed as transference rather than as treatment-related.

I concluded that multiple-role relationships tend to be emotionally incestuous, i.e., they are secretive, in that participants don't talk about them. And like other forms of incest they are an abuse of power. They exploit the vulnerability of those in a dependent position.[3]

I had made the same point in a brief article (Pepper, 1989). It was published as part of the Reader's Forum in an edition of the American Group Psychotherapy's Association's *International Journal of Group Psychotherapy* in January of 1989. It was written in response to an article by West and Livesley (1986) about the group therapist's transparency. Their argument was that group leaders who blur the boundaries of the "as if" relationship between leader and member do so in order to feed their own hunger for emotional gratification. This need stems from the leader's self-absorption, an unwillingness or inability to tolerate the deprivation that maintaining the frame entails. Group members are objects. The leader does not see them as separate from him or her, in need of the safety of a secure frame. The group exists to satisfy the leader's narcissism.

It occurred to me that the establishment of dual relationships at training institutes was a potentially hazardous special case of the therapist's transparency. I wrote at that time, "If the group colludes with the senior therapist to protect his narcissism, then those patient/therapists who are privy to knowledge about the leader that is neither accessible to others nor flattering to the leader may be in danger. These patient/therapists can be made to feel crazy if their perceptions of reality are consistently invalidated" (Pepper, 1989, p. 128).

Since that time, there has been a growing list of books and articles on the subject (Dorpat, 1996; Kirsner, 2000; Raubolt, 2006, Zur, 2001a, 2001b, 2009). In 2003, the journal *GROUP,* the publication of the Eastern Group Psychotherapy Society, devoted an entire issue to the subject. However, no one, to my knowledge, has taken my thesis further and developed an explanation of the connection between ego dysfunction and these complicated relationships. At the time of my original article, I reasoned that this was because clinicians did not see how dual relationships confounded the transference and countertransference. When leaders and their group members have pre-histories, the transference and countertransference are compromised. This was not an entirely new thought, though. Actually Freud (1910) said it first, though he didn't abide by his own rules of treatment, and then Fenichel (1974) developed it further thirty-five years later.

From a psychoanalytic perspective, the danger lies in the dilution of the transference through the blurring of boundaries. Multiple-role relationships breach the frame of the treatment, and the transference loses its specific character as a result (Fenichel, 1974). The senior group therapist who is socially involved with his or her patients loses valuable leverage to interpret all negative treatment reactions as transference. Since the integrity of the treatment is compromised, the distinction between reality and distortion that transference implies is not clear. As a result, negative treatment reactions cannot be assumed to be purely transference. If the patient is held responsible for all treatment impasses, then ego decompensation may occur (Temerlin & Temerlin, 1982).

The thesis, simply said yet not readily recognized by participants in the training process, is twofold: 1) that in order for group leaders to legitimately interpret negative treatment reactions as distortion, the frame of treatment has to be secure. Therefore it follows that the incidence of ego dysfunction of some group therapists trained at analytic institutes may be related to the group therapist's participation in multiple-role relationships with his or her own group therapist and fellow group patients affiliated with the same institute. Further, the incestuous nature of these relationships may obfuscate a clear view of their impact and thereby do harm; and 2) the natural insulation afforded the leader by virtue of that role, coupled with the leader's own narcissism, protects the leader from the damage of these relationships. Sadly, it is the patient/member who must bear the brunt of blurred boundaries in treatment. This is particularly the case when the patient/trainee's negative treatment reactions are interpreted as transference when in fact they are not.

Apparently, this blind spot still exists in the profession, as evidenced by the example in the first chapter in which my peer supervision group did not see the connection, in a case presented by one of our members, between his therapy group member's negative treatment reaction and the fact that he was also her boss. The peer group was adamant and unanimous that her negative reaction was a distortion and not a reaction to her compromised treatment. The following incident is another case in point, this time a flagrant one. Here again, though, the original publication of this event was written from the position of an unidentified observer. I was that observer.

At a conference of therapists, sponsored by the Center for Modern Psychoanalytic Studies, a group therapist presented a difficult case before an audience of over two hundred clinicians. The problem dealt with the management of the intractable negative transference of a female patient. In the course of the case presentation, the therapist noted that the woman, who was also a therapist, was seated in the audience several rows away from him. From the stage, Phyllis Meadow asked the woman to stand up and identify herself. Wisely, the woman declined to do either.

Nevertheless, the presenting therapist proceeded to describe his understanding of the dynamics of the case and the nature of her resistance to treatment. The panel of experts on the stage, which included Lou Ormont and Leslie Rosenthal, suggested strategies to best manage the case. No one suggested that perhaps the negative transference was related to the therapist's (and for that matter the entire organization's) lack of regard for appropriate boundaries. Equally disturbing was that *neither the presenting therapist, nor any of the experts, nor anyone in the audience, including myself, addressed the ethics of identifying a patient in public.*

If I hadn't witnessed it, I would not have believed it possible. But it was a potent reminder of the power of group pressure that I subsequently came to understand as the conspiracy of silence that surrounds the concealment, in some circles, of talking about the impact of dual relationships.

The moral of this story is that there is no safety in numbers. As it turned out, I wasn't the only one who was intimated by that experience. When I decided to sublimate my indignation about what I had witnessed by writing about it and then submitting the article for publication to a prestigious journal in the profession, the paper was rejected. The editor said that *I* was violating the confidentiality of conference participants. This was a public event. "Whose confidentiality did I violate?" I asked. I didn't receive a response. Apparently, the editor was paranoid about being sued. But it drove home again the thought that a conspiracy of silence prevailed when it came to openly addressing boundary issues in group therapy.

Dual-Role Relationships: A Very Brief History

The issue of blurred boundaries at training institutes is not a new one. Research tends to indicate that some incidence of omnipotent therapists who flaunt rules of extra-treatment contact, setting, and raising fees, referrals to patient/colleagues, advice giving, and all manner of questionable practices has been around for a long time (Dulchin & Siegel, 1982; Fenichel, 1974; Kirsner, 2000; Pepper, 1990, 1996; Roazen, 1974; Temerlin & Temerlin, 1982). Its roots reach back to Freud's establishment of the first training institute.

The history of secure-frame violations goes all the way back to the beginning of the psychoanalytic movement. As others have noted (Kirsner, 2000; Roazen, 1974), Freud himself was not particularly Freudian when it came to the way he ran his practice. That Freud analyzed his own daughter, vacationed with patients, and generally did not adhere to his own rules of analysis is widely known. As Roazen (1974) has noted:

> From Freud's point of view, there were good reasons for doing what he did. The rules he set down in his papers were not intended for himself, and he did not expect his students to follow them too closely either. (p. 439)

The institutionalization of blurred boundaries originated with Freud. He disdained academia, and so created a free-standing training institute. This gave rise to the establishment of a social environment in which emotionally incestuous relationships flourished (Kirsner, 2000), relationships that have come to be known as multiple-role or dual relationships.

Probably the first incident of an iatrogenic treatment reaction caused by dual relationships comes from within Freud's own inner circle. It occurred between Victor Tausk, Freud's student and intellectual rival, and Helene Deutsch, also Freud's patient and student, and a colleague of Tausk. Freud's view that countertransference is "what arises in the physician as a result of the patient's influence on his unconscious feelings" (Freud, 1910, p. 144) may have shielded him from having to accept some responsibility for compromising the treatment of both Tausk and Deutsch, and for precipitating Tausk's suicide.

Freud may have been threatened by his junior colleague's competitive attitude toward him. So when Tausk asked Freud to analyze him, Freud refused. Instead, Freud referred Tausk to Helene Deutsch. Tausk reluctantly accepted this emasculating position. The unspoken message was clear. Freud favored Deutsch over him. Freud finally put his foot down when he learned that Tausk had used his sessions with Deutsch to complain about him and Deutsch, in turn, used her sessions with Freud to complain about Tausk (so much for confidentiality). When Freud decided to call a halt to this triangle, he gave Deutsch an ultimatum to terminate treatment with Tausk or end her analysis with him.

Not surprisingly, she terminated treatment with Tausk (Pepper, 1996). Shortly thereafter, Tausk committed suicide. However, Tausk was no angel himself. At the time of his death, he was engaged to a female patient of his. Clearly, Tausk's troubles were not all Freud's doing. At the same time, Freud's behavior was deleterious to both Deutsch and Tausk. That Tausk took Freud's lead and also created dual relationships with patients could be viewed as the first case of dumping, or the pass-along effect, in which the senior therapist passes his pathology onto his subordinates, who then act out themselves (see Chapter 5. This is one of the seven dangers to be discussed in that chapter).

That Freud took no responsibility at all for Tausk's death was revealed in a letter to a friend about Tausk, where he wrote, "I confess I do not really miss him: I had long taken him as useless, indeed a threat to the future" (quoted in Roazen. 1974, p. 321).

Surely, both Tausk and Deutsch were ultimately responsible for their own choices. One can only imagine the enormous pull toward unconscious gratification that must have been exerted so close to the "master's feet." The wish to be emotionally fed by Freud, coupled with the fear of displeasing him, may have blinded both Deutsch and Tausk to the dangers of blurred boundaries. The seductiveness of these types of incestuous relationships is repeated time and again throughout the history of training institutes.

THE PROS: IN DEFENSE OF DUAL RELATIONSHIPS

One of the more controversial subjects in the field of psychotherapy today is the topic of dual relationships in practice. As noted earlier, some professional codes of ethics have deemed dual relationships to be unethical.[4] However, there are some practitioners who avidly defend their use. Notably, Ofer Zur (2001a, 2001b, 2009) is one of the most outspoken proponents of dual relationships in individual psychotherapy. In recent years, he has written books, articles, given talks, and created a website to publicize his point of view. While I have publicly taken issue with him on this matter, and I have questioned his assumptions about the legitimacy of dual relationships, they may have some merit.

As an aside, we first met back in 2001 at an APA Conference in San Francisco, after having sparred in print for some years; he told me that he was surprised by my appearance. I asked him why. He said that he was expecting me to look like an old fogey for having given him a tough time about blurred boundaries. I was surprised that he would resort to an *ad hominem* argument to support his views, but I was even more unpleasantly surprised to read, in his rejoinder to a published disagreement with him: "I doubt that Fenichel and Dr. Pepper have had extensive actual experience with dual relationships that can lead to an empirically based expert assessment of the issue" (Zur, 2001a, p. 203).

The reality is, of course, that this book was written, in part, because of my personal experience with complicated dual relationships. On one hand, I took umbrage with his arrogant presumption. On the other hand, I was flattered that Dr. Zur placed me in the company of Dr. Fenichel. In any event, I do agree with Dr. Zur when he writes that dual relationships may be beneficial under certain circumstances.

He says: "Dual relationships and familiarity do not nullify transference work but only make it more reality, rather than imagination or idealization, based" (Zur, 2009, p. 56). However, I believe that benefits are limited to only cases of over-idealization of the therapist.

For example, dual relationships can help to de-mystify an overly idealized transference. A patient who has been in treatment with the same practitioner for many years and who has not moved beyond the positive transference may need help seeing the therapist's shortcomings in order to resolve this resistance to growth (Chessick, 1974). A neurotic patient who has placed his therapist on a pedestal actually might benefit from seeing the therapist as a real person, warts and all. Establishing an extra-treatment relationship with this type of patient might have a therapeutic purpose, if the decision to introduce the patient into a dual relationship is a deliberate and conscious effort on the clinician's part to de-mystify himself or herself. If it were in the patient's best interest to do so, then a dual relationship would be therapeutic

(Pepper, 1990, p. 152). However, dual relationships can be hazardous for group members who have a weak grasp of reality.

For example, the pre-oedipal group member[5] has a characterological problem with boundaries. "They are prone to acting out and need clearly defined limits" (Ormont, 2001, p. 84). Dual relationships for this type of group member can be disruptive to their weak egos. In analytic group psychotherapy, the multiple transferences are often intense, and can precipitate a crisis for the pre-oedipal member, even in a secure frame milieu. Consequently, dual relationships are a liability for them and the dangers clearly outweigh the benefits. Part of my disagreement with Dr. Zur centers on our differing conceptualization of transference (Pepper, 2001a).

In discussing Freud's definition of transference, Racker (1987) notes: "Freud denominated '*transference*' the entirety of the patient's psychological phenomena and processes referred to the analyst and derived from other, previous object relations" (Racker, 1987, p. 13). From an analytic perspective, the negative transference is the patient's distorted perception of the therapist based on the patient's past.

Dr.Zur's concept of working with transference appears to run counter to the analytic view, although he claims to work analytically. In his view, transference can be corrected through dual relationships. This seems contrary to the concept of analytic work with transference, which calls for the clinician's understanding of the distorted perception rather than attempting to modify it. As noted earlier, the clinician's effort to deliberately change a member's perception of him or her may do more harm than good. This intervention would be contraindicated with borderline, schizophrenic, and psychotic group members whose wobbly defenses could be toppled by any attempt to alter them.

Transference is a resistance. It is a defense against the experience of spontaneous feelings in the here and now, and like all defenses it serves an adaptive purpose. Defenses allow the group member to function, stabilizing the member's fragile ego, but at a cost. The cost is the patient's symptomatology. Transference is an unconscious compromise solution, protecting the group member from acting on the strong aggressive and libidinal drives toward the object.

That certainly was true in Sonny's case where he protected the group leader at his own expense. When the boundaries are blurred and the patient has a social relationship with the therapist, often the patient feels a sense of gratification from this unique connection, a connection that is both overstimulating and inhibiting, and another aspect of the conspiracy of silence (for an example, see Chapter 5, the section on overstimulation).

Inadvertently, the establishment of dual relationships may create an environment in which verbalizing negative feelings toward the therapist is even more difficult for the patient than an environment in which the boundaries are clearly defined. Patients, for example, may fear revealing negative emotions lest they jeopardize their special closeness to the therapist. However, the problem with dual relations may be not only the inhibition of negative feelings. The therapist's objectivity is compromised when boundaries are blurred as well. In other words, it is not just the transference that may be in jeopardy here. The countertransference can be affected too. Fenichel (1974) noted that in the case of dual relationships *both* the transference and the countertransference lose their specific character.

Dr. Zur tells the reader of a patient's negative response to having attended a Chanukah party at Dr. Zur's home. He says that this was an instance of a negative transference (Zur, 2001a). While it's true that every relationship has at least some element of transference, when the boundary between therapy and not-therapy is blurred then it is impossible to know if the patient's perception is a distortion.

Once Dr. Zur has made therapy into not-therapy and the boundary is breached, Dr. Zur can no longer assert with any certainty what the reality is. A consequence of inviting a patient to be guest at his party has been to introduce a measure of uncontrolled stimulation to the equation. Who knows what the patient was responding to? Could it be that the patient caught Dr. Zur cheating at "dreidel"? However, at least one other clinician seems to share Dr. Zur's view of transference.

A colleague who runs many weekly groups and who engages in dual relationships with members has told me that outside-the-group contact helps members overcome the negative transference to him. He has told me that if a patient sees him as cold and uncaring in the treatment setting, then they are corrected of that perception when they see him socially and realize that he is actually quite the opposite, warm and caring.

This view of negative transference seems to echo Dr. Zur's. Both these clinicians seem to think that dual relationships make the negative transference reality-based. The task of analytic group treatment is not to correct the members' perceptions of the leader by seeing the real person outside the group but to resolve the negative feelings by the open airing of them and then organically working through them in the group process.

If transference is viewed as a resistance, then dual relationships, which are a special case of an altered-frame milieu, rigidify the group members' defenses by overwhelming them. The group is overstimulated by their social interaction with each other and with the leader, and is unable to differentiate which emotions arise from the present group interactions and which emotions are historical derivatives. The treatment environment is so compromised that it cannot be trusted to sort out reality from distortion.

We know from physics that energy can neither be created nor destroyed; it can only change form. The same is true for emotions. As a consequence, group members in a blurred boundary environment are left with a choice of three unenviable options: 1. act out the confusion of emotions in their real lives; 2. act in the emotions in the treatment group; or 3. turn the emotions back onto themselves in the form of symptoms. The conspiracy of silence prohibits an open discussion of the members' dilemma of knowing what is real.

Despite all this evidence, it has been my impression from my discussions with Dr. Zur and my colleague that they both sincerely believe in the value of these relationships. However, it is also my impression that otherwise bright, psychologically sophisticated, and ethical practitioners who engage in dual relationships have not fully thought through the ramifications carefully enough. As a result, Dr. Zur and others may have developed a blind spot that obscures their perception of the untoward, and unintended, consequences of dual relationships.

Marty Livingston, too, argues that dual relationships with charismatic leaders can be a positive force. He adds, almost as an aside, though, that this constructive energy comes with "some pitfalls" (Livingston, 2006, p. 84). This is an understatement. The pitfalls for Livingston, as it turns out, are quite formidable and destructive indeed. According to Livingston, his mentor, who was also his individual and group therapist, and key administrator, was often verbally abusive to him. Livingston admits to feeling traumatized by these verbal attacks. And yet, despite his acknowledgment that the "boundaries were quite blurred," and that he was often left feeling emotionally shattered by the sadistic and mean-spirited denigration of him, Livingston appears to rationalize his reaction to the abuse as a breakthrough. He turned the experience completely around and said that his relationship with this man was a growth experience. This obfuscation reminds me of the pattern of mind control that Dutton and Painter (1985) describe in cases of domestic violence where the passivity of the abused is so complete and self-esteem is so eroded that he or she believes that the abuse is for the good, making her or him stronger.

Abused partners often experience an *intensification* of attachment to the abuser after an episode of mistreatment. This is known as "traumatic bonding" (Dutton & Painter, 1985). The erosion of self-esteem that results from abuse heightens the victim's sense of dependency. This produces an increase in the power discrepancy between the abused and abuser that sharpens the isolation and despair of the victim and leads to an increase in masochistic clinging.

My snooping side would love to know how Livingston prevented the toxicity of his dual relationship with his therapist from seeping into his own practice. In any event, I have come to the conclusion that, more often than not, the costs of dual relationships outweigh their benefits.

NOTES

1. Ironically, the American Group Psychotherapy Association's ethics guidelines are vague about dual relationships (AGPA, 1999)

2. This is reminiscent of the famous Zimbardo (2007) prisoner–guard experiment at Stanford.

3. There are some cases in which sexual contact does occur, but these appear to be less likely than in individual therapy (Vinogradov & Yalom, 1989).

4. See the APA Code of Ethics (1992) and the Federation of Clinical Social Worker's Code of Ethics (1997).

5. Ormont (2001) defines the preoedipal patient as "those we commonly call the borderline, the schizoid, and the orally regressed" (p. 137).

Chapter Three

The Intrapersonal, Interpersonal, and Systemic Forces of Cult-Like Group Training Institutes

The People Who Populate Them

THE INSTITUTE LEADERS

What motivates some senior institute leaders to knowingly engage in treatment practices that run counter to the knowledge and wisdom in the profession? What are they thinking? How do they justify their behavior to themselves? Gabbard & Lester (1995) say that only a very small minority are actually sociopaths (I assume Gabbard believes they are mostly men), predators (sexual or not) who have no conscience and care nothing for the pain they cause and the damage they inflict on others. According to Gabbard, the majority are narcissistic, arrogant, and greedy. Since Gabbard provides only anecdotal data, we will have to take his word for the percentages for each category that he describes. My unrepresentative sample, however, does seem to confirm his findings, closely resembling Gabbard's description of this type of clinician.

In previous papers (Pepper, 2013, 2014a), I have suggested that most senior leaders who blur boundaries are not pathological. Among the ones who do blur boundaries, there are many who suffer a blind spot when it comes to understanding the dangers of dual relationships. For example, one senior institute clinician actually told me that his patients feel flattered when he invites them to join his training program. He and others delude themselves into thinking that anything short of sexual contact goes, as long as the patient says everything (Pepper, 1991). But we know from clinical experience that patients don't say everything, even under ideal conditions.

Apparently, these clinicians believe that they are so well analyzed and psychologically sophisticated that they can discard the wisdom and ethics of the field without consequence. In their minds, their great awareness justifies ignoring the literature on transference and countertransference. At best this attitude is naïve; at worst it can be dangerous. To believe that one is beyond the dangers of blurred boundaries simply by virtue of one's brilliance is an act of hubris (Pepper, 1991). Hubris is a form of arrogance based on insecurity. Some have gone so far as to put it in writing. We can get some sense of the personalities and the way of thinking of clinicians of this ilk through their books and articles.

For example, Richard Kramer (1987) penned an article about the resolution of his rage toward his parents by treating them. He justifies his decision to analyze his parents by quoting Freud (1913), who wrote that "no analyst would refuse his help to persons for whom no other help is accessible" (p. 115). I find it both amusing and telling that Kramer omits the last sentence of that famous quote: "He has only to know that in doing so he takes the risk of losing his friends" (quoted in Fenichel, 1974, p. 580). Others, like Kramer, have used Freud's quote as a rationalization too.

First, it is debatable whether no other help was available. Second, in such a contaminated treatment environment as this is, the therapist's motivation for treating his parents is murky at best. Just as the transference has "an analytically uncontrolled prehistory" (Fenichel, 1974, p. 580), so does the countertransference. How would Kramer be sure that his own unconscious and destructive impulses are not in play, counterbalancing his conscious desire to help (Pepper, 1991)?

In another instance, at the very end of an article by Evelyn Liegner (1984), "Countertransference in the Treatment of Friends and Relatives," where she describes her treatment of close relatives, she lets the reader in on her guilt and self-doubt about what she has done, despite reassurances from her kin. She says that her patient/relatives have reassured her "that God will not strike me dead for my hubris" (Liegner, 1984, p. 169).

In part, egregious violations of the frame of analytic group treatment may be explained by the leader's insensitivity to the effects of blurred boundaries. This may be related to the character structure of the individual. Maeder (1989) studied the family background of "wounded healers" and found that their families were characterized by "mothers who were pallid and uninspired…fathers were typically weak and estranged, though their children admired them" (p. 39).

My research (Pepper, 1990, 1991, 1996, 2004b) tends to indicate that the leader's narcissism is at the heart of the problem. Grandiose, authoritarian group therapists tend to be self-absorbed. As such, they are capable of treating group members like objects, as extensions of themselves, to be used to gratify the leader's needs first.

A characterological lack of empathy allows these leaders to exploit the members' dependency by bending the rules of treatment through such practices as creating dual relationships, using subjective criteria to determine fee increases, overloading the group with too many members, and, in general, by taking advantage of members' attachment to the leader and to each other. There is no consideration of the group's need for the safety of a secure frame environment. The leader is capable of the objectification of his patients, and the treatment becomes abusive.

For example, experts in the field have written that the optimal group size is between five and ten (Yalom, 2005, p. 292), thus providing members with the opportunity for face-to-face interactions with each other during each group session. However, some unscrupulous leaders have overfilled their groups with upward of twenty to twenty-five members. It has been reported to me that in response to a complaint about group size, one such leader teased that she intended to build a balcony to accommodate even more (personal communication to the writer).

In another instance, a member confronted an authoritarian group leader who had raised the fee twice, for a total of 25 percent, within a two-year period. The member said that such raises were arbitrary and offensive. They were not reflective of increases determined by objective criteria like inflation, cost of living, or changes in the leader's training and expertise. He accused the leader of being greedy. In response, the leader said, "You have a choice; you can leave."

This remark humiliated the member and silenced the group. Not only had the leader created an ethical violation by threatening abandonment of treatment, but tacitly told the group that he saw them as things, demonstrating a stunning lack of empathy toward the group and its members. In suggesting that the offending member could leave, he showed a lack of regard for the emotional connection that members had to each other. Leaving the group would mean severing ties with them as well as with the leader. This group therapist had a captive audience. He misused the members' dependency needs to gratify his greed. The fee increases, in this context, can be seen as an abuse of power (Pepper, 2004b).

Mullan (1987) has written that practitioners of group therapy cannot be unethical and provide competent group therapy. His research tends to indicate that, independent of degree and type of training, the outcome of treatment is directly related to the character structure of the practitioner. "The excellence, art and goodness of therapy reside in the person of the therapist and are only secondarily to be found in her skill, technique and role" (Mullan, 1987, p. 408). When entering treatment, the patient must assume that the therapist is "of goodwill, neither willingly abusing nor exploiting their patient" (Mullan, 1987, p. 404).

It would be frightening to think otherwise, and yet this is not always the case. As Langs (1982) notes, there are therapists who, consciously or not, harbor destructive attitudes toward their patients. I have often wondered if a therapist can behave unethically and still function therapeutically. If a therapist is doing "bad" things, can they be trusted to make decisions that are in the patient's best interest? I think not. It is my belief that the practice of therapy reflects the clinician's way of life (Pepper, 1991).

More than once, patients of mine have asked me to treat a relative of theirs but bill the insurance company under their name. When I refuse they often say, "Who would know?" My reply is always the same: "You and I would know." The message is clear. Colluding with them to defraud the insurance company would not only be illegal, but it would also undermine their treatment.

The following is an instance of a therapist who, as a writer of case histories from his practice, reveals the type of thinking of clinicians who deliberately blur boundaries. And once again, when this was originally published, I wrote it from the perspective of an outside observer (Pepper, 1996). In the spirit of transparency, I was more than just an outside observer and there is a backstory that I'd like to disclose.

Years ago, a former girlfriend of mine entered individual treatment with George Weinberg. She adored him and she urged me to read his books. I was jealous of her attachment to him and dragged my feet about reading his publications. My attitude changed, however, after she told me that he had advised her to break off her relationship with me. According to her, he said that I was "dangerous to her." While she assured me that no one would dictate how to run her affairs, she left me soon thereafter. It was then that I decided to read his books.

In the preface to *The Taboo Scarf,* Weinberg acknowledges the need to protect the confidentiality of patients that he writes about in this case study collection. To quote: "I have altered the stories to make them unrecognizable" (Weinberg, 1990, p. vii). However, he reveals his personal connection to a patient. He tells the reader that a former girlfriend, Susan, has asked him to treat her offspring; the depressed young woman in the chapter entitled "The Beacon" is actually his ex's daughter. In identifying his relationship to the patient's mother, he blows the cover off his commitment to protecting the confidentiality of both of them. The negative effects of this wild arrangement for the poor patient are apparent in her first session (Pepper, 1996, pp. 290-292).

The patient, Lisa, makes what seems to be an oblique reference to him: "I hate doctors" (Weinberg, 1990, p. 12). Weinberg attempts to reassure her that he only wants to help, but apparently misses the unspoken message of Lisa's communication to him.

My interpretation of these events is consistent with Robert Langs's theory of *deviant frame therapy* (Langs, 1989). Langs believes that patients are sensitive to frame violations but are not necessarily able to directly respond to them. Instead, patients communicate their feelings symbolically through encoded dreams and messages.

Lisa asks him, "Did you know that termites, when they're under attack, create more soldiers than usual? In one week, they give birth to ten percent warrior termites instead of two" (Weinberg, 1990, p. 14). He encourages Lisa to describe the details of the termite behavior, thinking that it is a metaphor for Lisa's relationship to her mother, who is characterized as the "queen termite."

Another interpretation would be that Lisa's presentation is an example of what Langs calls *iatrogenic paranoia,* "which is reflected in stories of spies, intruders, unwanted company, inept people who can't function for themselves and so on" (Langs, 1989, p. 123). Weinberg appears to confirm this hypothesis when he presses Lisa for details of Susan's life.

But perhaps the most telling revelation of his character appears in his explanation of why he agreed to give Lisa money to treat her sick cat. Weinberg responds to his unseen critics with an *ad hominem* argument. Rather than defend his position on a firm theoretical basis, Weinberg justifies his behavior by contemptuously dismissing ethical practitioners as "despicable precisionists" with character flaws:

> It has never crossed my mind that my offer of money would have any countertherapeutic element. How despicable are the precisionists in psychology who care more about the operation than the patient! (Weinberg, 1990, p. 25).

By claiming moral superiority, Weinberg overlooks the iatrogenic consequences of giving money. The act of gift giving may be viewed as a form of projective identification. Langs (1982) has labelled this *dumping*, or what I have called the *pass-along effect*, another of the seven dangers to be discussed in Chapter 5.

In a more extreme form, Gabbard & Lester (1995) describe the character structure of grandiose clinicians who rise to the top of their profession in individual psychotherapy. Gabbard's description very much matches my own earlier description (Pepper, 1990, 1991, 1992) of group therapy institute leaders (albeit they are not necessarily sexual predators), who nevertheless blur treatment boundaries through nonsexual dual relationships.

They also identify another of the seven dangers as it applies to training institutes for individual psychotherapy. He writes: "The idealization of senior colleagues may create situations reminiscent of the fairy tale *The Emperor's*

New Clothes, in which otherwise intelligent analysts disbelieve or rationalize what they see in plain view" (Gabbard & Lester, 1995, p. 95). To quote:

> He may be in a position of major responsibility…he may be internationally renowned for his writing, or he may be a revered teacher. The adulation he receives is intoxicating to the point that he begins to believe that he is different from and superior to others. His grandiosity is fueled, and he begins to rationalize his boundary-less behavior as acceptable simply because of who he is. Ordinary standards of ethics do not apply to him. (Gabbard & Lester, 1995, p. 94).

For example, some time ago, I was asked by a well-known group therapist to sit in as an ethics consultant on the beginning phase of the development of a group training institute under his leadership, based on his own unique brand of theory and technique. When the discussion came around to the subject of dual relationships, I made a case for the separation of teaching from treatment, carefully explaining the inherent dangers of merging these two functions, both as a potential source of contamination to the transference and, by definition, a breach of confidentiality. The leader summarily dismissed my concerns. He said that since he was trained and analyzed by the same therapists, he saw no problem in continuing that tradition. Organizations often justify the status quo by saying: "that's the way it's always been." Psychoanalytic training institutes are no exception; and that was the end of the discussion. It occurred to me, at that time, that the culture of group therapists may resist accepting that there is a discrepancy between reality and their beliefs.

Gabbard's depiction also appears to accurately reflect the character of my own individual/group therapist supervisor/teacher/buddy. He was also a charismatic, grandiose, authoritarian leader. Once again, when I originally published this vignette, I wrote in the third person, but it actually happened to me (Pepper, 1991).

In a bizarre role reversal, my group therapist told me a dream that he had. Initially, I believed his motivation for telling me his dream was self-serving, to show how psychologically sophisticated he was, but in reality he revealed more about himself and our relationship than he consciously knew. Here is his dream.

> I am standing to the side of a road in the middle of the night watching people in my life walk single file into a cave. They all appear to be in a trance. At the entrance of the cave stands the devil leading them away. The devil approaches me and says, "You are different from the rest. You are too smart to follow me blindly as the others do." (Pepper, 1991, p. 68)

At the time I wrote this, I used the dream to illustrate the simultaneous brilliance and tragic flaw of the grandiose, narcissistic therapist. I said that when the dreamer awakes he realizes that the devil's flattery is a seduction. To believe that he is "too smart" to be fooled by the devil is the devil's attempt to fool him. For a moment, he is fully conscious, for the dreamer understands that the devil seduces by appealing to his narcissism. But the awareness doesn't last because it doesn't stop the grandiose therapist from acting out his arrogance in life.

His belief that he is so conscious that he can violate the rules of secure analytic treatment is then his own self-deception. Falling victim to his own delusions of grandeur, he is seduced by the devil within. It is an act of hubris to believe that one is beyond danger common to others simply by virtue of one's brilliance. The narcissistic therapist is blinded by the glare of his own faulty internal logic. By turning a blind spot into a virtue, the narcissistic leader deludes himself into thinking that he is beyond the need for external feedback (Slater, 1974). And by denying his own dependency needs, he denies his own humanness. This is his tragic flaw.

In denying these needs, the grandiose leader may unwittingly foster the development of a pathological dependency on him through the establishment of dual relationships with patients. The patient/trainee acts out the leader's split-off and denied dependency needs. A process of projective identification, similar to Scharf's description of couples (Scharf, 1986) emerges, in which the patient denies his or her own strength and power and lives vicariously through the apparently strong leader. An unconscious collusion ensues, which is simultaneously chaotic and binding, preventing the patient from individuating and leaving the fold. At the time I wrote this, my conclusion was, "It was not uncommon, therefore, for treatment with the same analyst to last 10, 20, 25 years or more" (Pepper, 1991, p. 68).

In retrospect, I have wondered why he told me this dream in the first place. What was the unspoken message from him? Could it be that the dream was actually a warning to me about him, that *he* was the devil in the dream, and *I* was the one standing outside the cave? Was he telling me that *I* was too smart to follow him like others do?

THE PATIENT/TRAINEES

From the outset, it is important to acknowledge the seductiveness of dual relationships for the patient/trainee. The perceived benefits of such complicated entanglements are quite high; otherwise, how experienced professionals, who should know better, willingly compromise their treatment would seem unfathomable. Aside from the obvious gratification of "sitting at the master's feet," there are potent financial rewards as well. Some senior leaders refer patients to their patient/trainees. As a result, some patient/trainees have become successful as a direct result of their social involvement with their therapists. This is clearly a seductive but binding prize of the system. And yet, as we have seen in the last section, there are also some unscrupulous, psychopathic leaders who go well beyond narcissistic gratification and who sadistically exploit the dependency needs of emotionally damaged subordinates with, at times, catastrophic consequences (Pepper, 1990).

For example, Raubolt (2003, 2006) writes about a cult-like individual psychotherapy training institute from the perspective of a student/patient. He and others, in his collection of articles, focus on the personalities of those supervisors and patient/therapists who inhabit these places. In describing his own motivation for participating in an abusive supervisory/treatment relationship, he says that he was seduced by the initially warm welcome he received—good meals, fine wine, lively conversation. He says that he was treated like a king.

Obviously, no one is seduced against his will. Seduction implies complicity. Narcissistic gratification was a strong impetus for him. But I would venture to guess that there was more. In not taking full responsibility for the more basic and perhaps unconscious need to be taken care of by an apparently powerful authority figure, Raubolt may have missed the point.

In Fromm's (1941) *Escape from Freedom,* for example, the author describes the process by which people abdicate their own personal responsibility of freedom, one that engenders anxiety and uncertainty, in order to be taken care by a leader who promises safety. While his attention was directed at an attempt to explain how the good citizens of Germany, under Hitler, could behave so heinously, Fromm's conclusion had more general applications, as was revealed by Milgram's (1963) *Obedience* study.

Brothers (2003) refers to this process as "the intersubjective regulation of uncertainty" (p. 80). This principle seems similar for any protection contract. As Slater (1974) notes, eventually all protection contracts become protection rackets, as appears time and again throughout history and literature.

Dracula, for example, has power over only those who willingly allow him in. George Stade says in the introduction of an updated edition of the classic work, "But he [Dracula] cannot cross any threshold or any windowsill without an invitation from someone within who is responsive to his suit" (in Stoker, 1981, p. v). Goethe makes the same point in *Faust:* Who protects the followers from the protector once he shows himself to be the devil?

Livingston (2006), in his story of an abusive dual relationship with his therapist/supervisor, suggests that part of his attraction to this complicated relationship stems back to his childhood. Livingston's father died when he was quite young. It was his hunger for a strong authority figure that drove Livingston into this relationship. Apparently Livingston confused the man's strength with his sadism.[1] This pattern is reiterated with the development of dual relationships in cult-like institutes.

The Temerlins (1982) describe the family backgrounds of patient/therapists at the institutes that they studied. They found that one or both parents were either depressed and/or psychotic and, in some instances, alcoholic. The children were often cast in the role of family nurturer, since the parents were dysfunctional. In the institutes, they regressed.

I believe that this is a dynamic process that includes the trainee's active participation. To see themselves as victims, Raubolt and others overlook an important component of the problem. They are not prisoners. Much like the subjects in Zimbardo's famous experiment at Stanford, the "prisoners" were free to leave at any time. They chose not to (Zimbardo, 2007). The power of the group is such that it can obfuscate authenticity.

Under these conditions, the interactional dynamic of members' original family is re-created. As children of self-absorbed parents, the patient/trainee has been groomed to put their own needs aside in order to tend to the needs of their parent. They learn to have their own dependency needs gratified by caring for others; in essence, they need to be needed. That is how they get taken care of.

The group leader's objectification of them dovetails with their own family experience. It is ego-syntonic and feels natural to indulge the leader's egotism. It's a perfect fit but it subverts the treatment. The transference becomes reality that draws members into a repetition compulsion that ultimately deprives them of what they are seeking, to be cared for by an omnipotent and selfless parent.

The Temerlins observed the obsequious of this type of patient/trainee. To quote: "members identified with the leader: some emulated his dress, manner of speech and life style. . . . A common sight was a patient doing menial work for the therapist. . . . We sometimes would forget that these patients were practicing mental health professionals" (Temerlin & Temerlin, 1982, p. 132). This observation matches my own. Sometimes, the blurring of boundaries can reach almost comical proportions.

In a training group in which I participated, I witnessed a small subgroup of male patient/trainees walk into the group room carrying boxes of computer parts. The leader, who was also their group therapist, had purchased a new computer and these men had come to assemble it for her. Had the nature of their connection to her and to each other been any social configuration other than as patient/trainees, then the scene would not have been so bizarre. But here was a group of grown men, as patient/trainees, acting in the capacity of assistants to their own group therapist. *And once again, no one said anything about it, including me* (Pepper, 2007).

When a senior therapist engages in dual relationships, I believe they are obliged to be particularly vigilant for any ego dysfunction that occurs in patients after these relationships have begun. This is an added burden to the work and places considerably more responsibility on the therapist. If ego decompensation does occur during the course of treatment, this could be a signal to the alert practitioner that this untoward reaction may be more than negative transference. It can be an indication of the potential danger of an iatrogenic treatment reaction.

One consequence of dual relationships at analytic training institutes is that sibling rivalry at these institutes may be more than just transference. Patient/trainees may curry favor with the leader, partly to enhance their position within the larger organization. As real-life competitors, patient/trainees vie for the symbolic rewards of loyalty to the leader such as patient referrals, teaching, supervisory, and administrative positions, and opportunities to represent the institute at professional conferences (Pepper, 2004a). Rivalries often are enacted in the supervision groups as patient/trainees compete for the leader's attention and approbation. As a result, the boundary between reality and fantasy can become hopelessly blurred, and the transference becomes the reality.

It could be said that, in the incident cited above where the clinicians acted like assistants, they had demeaned themselves in order to have a special connection to the leader. Anyone in the group who had taken note of the absurdity of this situation might run the risk of being scapegoated, another of the seven dangers. Those objecting to this complicated scenario might have had the group's aggression, which should have been directed toward the leader, displaced onto them. As Ormont (1974) has noted, scapegoating is a group defense that protects the leader at the expense of a weaker member. The objector's perception would have been viewed as a distortion. In other words, rivalries are often interpreted as transference rather than as directly related to the group process itself. As a result, the patient/trainees are held responsible for the impasses that occur as a result of this boundary-less interaction system, and iatrogenic treatment reactions can occur (Pepper, 1990, 2002).

However, I do not believe that this dynamic is solely a matter of the pathological narcissism of individuals, at least as it applies to the cult-like training institutes of group therapy. I believe that the social structure of these organizations fosters the development of dual relationships that then serve as the formation for the development of iatrogenic treatment. Once institutionalized, this dynamic becomes part of the organization's normative culture. It takes on a life of its own, though no one is ever quite sure how it all started.

It should be noted that within the community of group training institutes, scenarios like this one are familiar. In fact, it is quite common for senior therapists to be socially involved with their patients, and for the patients to be involved with each other. The social structure of some group training institutes is defined largely by these relationships. The establishment of dual relationships at these institutes cuts across ideological and theoretical differences in the field and, as I have observed earlier, their iatrogenic effects are endemic to the profession (Pepper, 1990).

TO TEACH OR TO TREAT

The Inherent Conflict of Interests of the Social Structure of Training Institutes

Observers of organizations have long noted their tendency toward entropy (Postman & Weingartner, 1969). After a time, all systems tend to run down and there is, as well, an inherent move toward chaos and disintegration. This entropic pull can be fueled by a system's primary inclination to preserve itself. Often in contradiction to its openly stated goals, this need to survive may be ultimately destructive.

In a previous article (Pepper, 1992) I wrote that this principle applies to social systems in general, and in this case group psychotherapy training institutes specifically. Before launching into the discussion of the social structure of training institutes and their inherent contradictions, I would like to tell a brief side story of how I came to understand this phenomenon.

When I wrote an article about the issue of dual relationships and confidentiality (Pepper, 2004a), my intention was to address a fascinating and curious phenomenon in the profession. There seemed to be a discrepancy between the belief system of many practitioners about confidentiality and reality. Many of my colleagues publicly said that they believed that confidentiality existed in their conference institutes, workshops, training, and therapy groups when, in fact, many knew that it really didn't. People paid lip service to confidentiality but did not necessarily abide by the rule. I wondered why that was.

Around that time, I was browsing the $1 book racks on the street outside the Strand Bookstore in New York City when I came upon a book by Philip Slater that caught my eye. In the 1970s and 1980s, I had read his books (*The Pursuit of Loneliness, Earthwalk,* and *Wealth Addiction*) about the effects of societal values on interpersonal and intrapersonal functioning. Slater was brilliant. He was one social psychologist who understood the crippling and emotionally fragmenting effects of society's masculine and dehumanizing value system. My eye caught his name on the spine of a book on the rack, so I picked up the book, *Footholds,* which had a chapter entitled "Dualities." In it, he wrote about the inherent contradictions of social systems.

When there are inconsistencies between a group's belief system and reality, then reality is often overlooked so as to mitigate the effects of this conflict (Slater, 1977). This helped me to understand the discrepancy between the rules about confidentiality and the actual adherence to them. In the following scenario, in which reality and the group's belief system do not jibe, reality is trumped by the need for internal order.

In a recent article (Pepper, 2014a), I told a story of a patient/ trainee at an analytic institute who demurred about presenting very personal material in a group in which she had complicated dual relationships with the other members. It was not a secret that most of the members gossiped outside the group, but nonetheless members attempted to assuage her worries about the lack of confidentiality by reminding her of the rule about no outside contact. Despite their reassurance, she refused to share her highly charged emotions. In response, the group interpreted her refusal as evidence of a character flaw, her problem with emotional intimacy. After the session, she left feeling anxious and depressed (personal communication to the writer). This dialogue reminded me of a chapter in Lewis Carroll's *Alice in Wonderland.* The start of Alice's conversation with the March Hare around the table at the Mad Hatter's Tea Party is as follows:

> "Have some wine," the March Hare said in an encouraging tone.
> Alice looked all round the table, but there was nothing on it but tea. "I don't see any wine," she remarked.
> "There isn't any," said the March Hare.
> "Then it wasn't very civil of you to offer it," said Alice angrily.
> "It wasn't very civil of you to sit down without being invited," said the March Hare. (Carroll, 2004, p.79)

Slater noted another feature of social systems that explicated the conflict of interest between teaching and treatment at analytic institutes. It seemed obvious once he explained the phenomenon. Slater noted that, just as ambivalence is the root of individual motivation, contradictory needs are fundamental to social systems as well (Slater, 1977).

Then I had an "aha" moment. The irreconcilable goals between group analytic institutes' need to teach and their need to treat are part of an ongoing tension within these organizations, and that compromise solutions are just that. They are an attempt to accommodate, however inadequately, these two contradictory needs. The need to teach is educational; the need to treat is clinical. To put them together under the same roof contaminates both.

For example, a friend of mine told me that she had taken a didactic class, at an analytic institute that was run like a therapy group. The instructor told the students that they were to talk about their feelings toward each other. During one class session, a student lit into the instructor. In front of the class, she told the instructor that she (the student) was hurt and angry because she knew that the instructor didn't like her. In fact, she said, "You've never liked me." My friend was confused, because it sounded as if the teacher and student had a pre-history that had not been explained to the class. When another student attempted to intervene and come to the student's defense and said, "I can understand how you feel," the student shot back at her, "No, you don't. You have no idea what I'm talking about." The class was taken aback. My friend suspected that the student and teacher were in some type of dual relationship that got brought into the room. It was an unpleasant encounter, dropped without explanation or resolution. Here then is an example of the conflict between teaching and treatment at an analytic training institute. Which is it? Institutes can't have it both ways, even if they try. And what are the effects on student/patients?

Slater noted that there are a myriad of contradictory needs in social systems. "Every system needs change and stability, deviation and conformity, creation and destruction, cooperation and competition, individualism and collectivism" (Slater, 1977, p. 155). Now things started to fit together more clearly.

Take Dulchin & Siegel's (1982) article on confidentiality in an individual analytic institute, that was introduced in the previous chapter, for example. Her description of the institute's failed attempt to work out a compromise between the conflicting need for secure boundaries and a separation of the teaching from treatment on the one hand, and the need for fluidity of boundaries and overlapping of therapy and education on the other, made sense in light of Slater's theoretical model of the inherent dualities in all social systems. It also clarified Gabbard's (1995) attempt to explain the position that teaching and treatment should not overlap. He says, "Violation of educational boundaries…inevitably leads to a 'wild' analysis; the supervisor cannot and should not try to enter into the candidates conflicts or unconscious fantasy" (Gabbard& Lester, 1995, p. 169). If Slater is correct, and I believe that he is, then attempts to contain the repressed need can last for only just so long.

Dulchin & Siegel (1982) studied the evaluation process of therapists at a well-known East Coast analytic institute. Their observations revealed that confidentiality might have been an illusion at that organization. In an effort to circumscribe the negative impact of dual relationships, the institute developed a policy whereby senior therapists were prohibited from supervising their own patients. However, senior therapists were permitted to treat the supervisees of other senior therapists affiliated with the institute, and all senior therapists attended supervisors' meetings. As a consequence, the boundary between treatment and supervision remained blurred and there was the potential for breaches of confidentiality.

In their study, Dulchin and Siegal (1982) examined the subtle ways in which the privacy of patient/supervisees was compromised in the evaluation process during these supervisors' meetings. Despite the organization's clearly stated goal to protect confidentiality by the separation of the therapy from the supervision, senior therapists/supervisors routinely communicated their feelings and judgments about their own patients at these institute meetings. Although these communications were nonverbal and largely unconscious, they nonetheless had a profound effect on the status of patient/supervisees within the organization. Confidentiality was violated and the integrity of the treatment was undermined.

Dulchin & Siegel speculated that one function of these communications was to informally monitor the quality of trainees who passed through the institute, in this way preserving the reputation of the organization within the professional community. Clearly, this was a conflict of interest between the organization's ethical responsibility to its patient/supervisees and its need to assure its own survival. Interestingly, when questioned about this unspoken communication system, many senior therapists denied its existence.

It is my belief that group therapists may be harmed in another way when the institutes in which they are trained promulgate frame violations in their treatment. Fostering the establishment of multiple-role relationships at analytic group institutes contributes to the neophyte group therapist's failure to develop an awareness of the need to maintain a secure frame of treatment in their own practices. The security of the frame is a major component to ethically and clinically sound therapy (Langs, 1982). This is a serious blind spot in the training of group leaders. Some group institutes foster, support, and at times encourage egregious frame violations. Secondary gain gratification, for all participants in multiple-role relationships, is also a powerful force that drives the system.

Trainees at most analytic group institutes are required to be in treatment as a condition of their graduation. At some institutes, trainees are free to select any analytically oriented group therapist; at others, they are encouraged to select one from a list of recommended training group therapists who double as supervisors, teachers, and administrators of the organization. And at a number of institutes across the nation, trainees *must* be in group treatment with members of the senior staff with whom they are socially involved.

Training institutes promulgate such a practice for a variety of reasons. Some may argue that the prime motive is quality control, in order to assure a high level of training, supervision, and analysis, as in the Dulchin study. However, it is also likely that greed, self-preservation, and narcissistic gratification are closer to the unspoken forces that motivate behavior. Obviously, a training class is a ready-made source of new group patients for senior group leaders who are willing to exploit their subordinate's dependency needs. Unethical senior leaders can often sustain their practices on naïve and psychologically unsophisticated neophytes who feel flattered to be part of a therapeutic community where they can "sit at the master's feet," and perhaps be granted some of the extras of the system like referrals, teaching, and administrative positions. Patient/trainees are often competitors, vying for these symbolic rewards of loyalty to the leader (Pepper, 1992).

Unlike other professions where the skill of the practitioner is taught in an academic setting, the art of the group therapist is taught in the emotional environment of transference and countertransference. Even under the ideal conditions of the separation of the treatment from the training, there is a large element of subjectivity that permeates the learning experience.

Kirsner (2000) notes that this leads to the inevitable idealization of the master teachers and the concomitant denigration of others. However, when the stakes are so high in a blurred-boundary environment, the denigration is often split off and displaced onto master teachers of other, competing training institutes. The process of anointment, where future teachers are culled from the training classes, is further complicated when the teachers and the training institute's group therapists are the same people.

Institutes that are built around a charismatic figure tend to view his theories and methods as truths. In doing so, however, the reverence becomes more like religious proselytizing than scientific validated fact (Kirsner, 2000). In the field of psychotherapy, the theories and methods do not lend themselves very well to scientific validation and quantification. But there is a paradoxical twist to this analysis.

I have observed, from over thirty-five years of clinical practice with difficult group members that certain modern analytic techniques, developed by charismatic, grandiose, and authoritarian leaders, actually work well with this population of group patients. And while it would be hard to scientifically demonstrate their effectiveness, they do tend to have heuristic value.

The reader may be surprised to learn that I believe that some modern analytic group techniques have worked successfully in my treatment of difficult group members. To my mind, there is a separation between the theory and the practice of modern analysis. I will have more to say about this apparent contradiction in later chapters.

Suffice it to say here that I have found that at least one of the tenets of modern theory, investigation rather than interpretation, has helped many of my severely damaged patients to heal. In my experience, borderline and schizophrenic group members often hear interpretations as narcissistic wounds, and they often have regressed to primitive levels of functioning when their behavior is interpreted to them, even if it is technically accurate. I believe this to be true because I have personally witnessed it time and again but, as I have just said, my arguments are anecdotal and as such do not stand up to strict scientific rigor.

Nevertheless, some modern institutes have promulgated these techniques as the *only* useful ones and are closed-minded to other ways of treatment. One leader of such an institute, for example, insisted that only his own patients could teach at his organization. Their journal mostly published articles written by adherents to the modern approach. However, there exists a group-think environment that, as the Temerlins (1982) and Kirsner (2000) point out, is not limited to the institutes of charismatic leaders but to the lesser ones as well.

The intensity of some analytic training institutes' need to survive at all costs, and the ferocity with which some of its senior staff defend it, even perhaps at the cost of trainees' well-being, was brought home to me in a particularly personal and rabid attack by a reviewer of an article on this subject that I had submitted for publication in a highly respected professional group journal. The reviewer wrote:

> This paper is a continuation of more than a decade and multiple papers in which the author takes a 'holier than thou' righteous position on what is actually a very complex situation. He does not consider the matter from the emotional and concrete needs of training programs. Has he graduated from a program or been on the faculty of a program and coped with the multiple demands of living in a real world and struggling to exist as a program?...and [what he] seems unaware of is that a high percentage of new students are recruited from the practices of faculty members. These candidates are attracted to training by their own therapeutic experiences rather than selfishly placed in faculty run groups.

The reviewer misses the point, and once again we see the use of an *ad hominem* argument. He does not seem to understand that the fact that new students are recruited from the practices of faculty members is precisely the problem. It does not matter whether trainees are in treatment with faculty/therapists before or after they begin training with them. What matters is that dual relationships exist at all. The vitriolic review of my article suggests that some training institute administrators are threatened by the thought of even considering the impact of dual relationships at these institutes. His recommendation ("My vote would strongly be to reject the article") would seem to point to a need to keep the whole thing quiet—another instance of the conspiracy of silence.

DISCUSSION

From the perspective of an outsider to the group psychoanalytic community, looking at the bizarre behavior presented in the above examples, one might rightly wonder why intelligent, mature, and psychoanalytically sophisticated people do not leave their institutes sooner than they do, if in fact they do at all. When leaders-in-training realize the mess they are in at these places and the destructive impact of their relationships, what stops them from immediately severing ties? The answer is rather complicated. Depending on the theoretical orientation of the writer, different interpretations are available.

Research has shown, for example, that groups can exert a strong regressive pull on members (Freud, 1921; Spotnitz, 1976). The dependency of the group on the leader can foster a childlike passivity. Motivated by a wish to be taken care of by a powerful parental figure, group members often abdicate their observing ego.

Organizational variables also play a role as well. There are at least three postulates about the nature of organizations that seem particularly significant in the study of the social structure of group training institutes and that make them ripe for the development of iatrogenic treatment reactions in their trainees: 1) All organizations tend toward entropy, a natural condition in the universe in which there is a predisposition for a system to run down, and there is, as well, an inherent pull toward chaos and disintegration (Postman & Weingartner, 1969); 2) All organizations exist to keep themselves in existence. As a consequence the entropic pull can be fueled by the system's primary inclination to preserve itself. Often in contradiction to its openly stated goals, this need to survive may ultimately be destructive and self-destructive; 3) Like individuals, organizations have contradictory needs. As a result there is often an inconsistency between an organization's belief system and its actual functioning (Slater, 1977).

The goal of this chapter has been to provide the reader with an overview of my thesis that alterations of the frame always have consequences for the treatment. While the primary focus so far has been the effects of dual relationships, the following chapters will include discussions of other frame alterations as well, and the seven dangers of blurred boundaries. The role of senior leader, coupled with the characteristically grandiose and authoritarian personality of many of these clinicians, shields them from the brunt of the damage of blurred boundaries. It is generally the patient/trainees who are at the greatest risk. The next chapter addresses the paradoxes of group treatment.

Dual relationships characterize the social structure of many training institutes and have done so from the beginning of the psychoanalytic movement. Freud himself violated his own rules about contact with patients outside the treatment. One consequence of Freud's disdain for academia, which led to his establishment of a free-standing institute, was the institutionalization of dual relationships. Dual relationships are by definition unethical, because they violate confidentiality.

As fewer group training institutes continue to survive in this era of economic hardship for the profession, and the positions of those that remain become more tenuous, it can be expected that unethical treatment practices will continue to exist unless professional organizations take a more active monitoring role.

If dual relationships are part of the social fabric of many group psychoanalytic institutes, then violations of the confidentiality of patient/trainees will be part of the process as well. The thesis of this chapter has been that the two are linked. However, this is not to say that there is nothing to be done about this serious limitation to the system.

One way to minimize the harmful effect of dual relationships on confidentiality is to talk about it. The Temerlins (1982) have noted that institutes run by charismatic, grandiose, and authoritarian leaders usually lack built-in external feedback systems, i.e., subgroups and/or individuals in positions of power within the organization who hold differing views from the leader. This feedback could possibly mitigate the effects of the blurring of reality. Slater (1974) has called the insular dynamic of narcissistic thinking of individuals' "inner circuitry" thinking, but it also applies to organizations as well, where it is called *group-think*. This is often seen in political circles, where leaders who are threatened by differences of opinion surround themselves with yes-men, simultaneously protecting them from other points of view but also blocking their view of reality, often with catastrophic consequences.

Professional organizations like the American Group Psychotherapy Association, and its affiliate organizations (like the Eastern Group Psychotherapy Society, the Northeastern Society for Group Psychotherapy, and the San Diego Group Psychotherapy Society), the American Psychological Association, the National Association of Social Workers, among others can raise the consciousness of practitioners by sponsoring talks, discussion groups, and workshops on the hazards of dual relationships on patient/trainee privacy. Despite the directive to do so, group members in blurred boundary environments don't say everything. It would be crazy to do so. The resolution of the dilemma of dual relationships, therefore, must come from within the profession but outside of the institutes themselves. Most institutes are too mired in their own internal dynamics and logic to see the problem clearly.

Even under ideal conditions of secure-frame therapy, members resist the process. However, in the case of a blurred boundary milieu, the conflict is not entirely an intrapsychic, characterological, one; but rather a sane reaction to the possibility of exposing oneself to danger. Group leaders can be made aware that the hesitancy of some members to reveal confidential information in group may not merely be a reflection of character pathology or transference. In fact, under certain conditions, it may be a healthy response to the possible peril of doing so in a treatment environment that is compromised.

NOTE

1. This point is also made in *Fearful Symmetry* (Novick & Novick, 1996) in their study of sadomasochism.

Chapter Four

Paradoxes in Group Psychotherapy

THE LEADER'S PARADOX: INSIGHT DOESN'T NECESSARILY HELP

It is my belief that, in order to function effectively as a leader in an analytic treatment group with difficult patients, a group therapist must feel comfortable with aggression, his own and that of the group and its members. The very nature of group elicits the aggression. The well-being of all participants demands that the leader metabolize this potentially volatile emotion and design interventions that facilitate the open airing of angry feelings without causing injury to any of the participants, himself or herself included. Needless to say, this can be a daunting task.

The various schools of analytic group psychotherapy differ in their approach to the treatment of aggression with pre-oedipal patients, the borderline and the schizophrenic members specifically. There is a great discrepancy between the traditional approach and the modern approach as to which type of intervention is best suited for this patient population. The traditional approach values awareness and understanding, employing interpretation as the intervention of choice.

Michels (1983) defines interpretation as "any intervention that aims to increase the patient's insight and understanding or to expand his or her awareness" (p. 61). But emotions are not of the intellect, particularly for the more disturbed group members. So I strongly disagree with Marvin Aronson, former director of the Group Training Program at the Post-Graduate Center, who stated: "The group format facilitates the therapist's interpretations.... It has long been recognized that accurate, well-timed interpretations of projective material constitute invaluable tools in the treatment of borderline and schizophrenic patients" (Aronson, 1977, p. 41). My thirty-plus years of running analytic treatment groups have shown just the opposite to be the case. In fact, many group members experience interpretations as an abusive attack, a narcissistic injury, and have become destabilized as a result. For instance, one year as a therapist trainee I had a classically trained supervisor advise me to interpret a male paranoid, homicidal schizophrenic's gift of a Coca-Cola bottle as a phallic symbol. Had I listened, the poor fellow might have had to kill me just to prove the point that he was not queer.

In an extreme and disturbing case, a young man, whose older brother was killed in a car accident, came to see me for a second-opinion consultation after his psychiatrist, who was medicating him with antidepressants, interpreted his reactive depression to his brother's death as a result of his guilt over feelings of sibling rivalry. The psychiatrist told him that he was depressed because he had unconsciously wished his brother dead. The poor young man was almost suicidal after hearing this. I reassured him that the psychiatrist was wrong and that his depression was a normal reaction to the traumatic loss of his beloved brother.

In another instance, a classically trained supervisor, who didn't seem to know how to deal with pre-oedipal aggression, recommended that I say "What else is new?" to a borderline member who told me one too many times in group that she was in a rage toward me. I knew enough even then that to say such a thing might have precipitated a psychotic break in her.

The modern analysts know that the key to working with this population is an understanding of the emotions that underlie behavior, rather than intellectual awareness. "What this theory of insight ignored was that character structure forms largely during those years when there were no words, no verbal thoughts, only impulses and feelings" (Ormont, 2001, p. 287). He further states: "We are especially interested in the feelings that lie behind acts, or that accompany acts, rather than in the reasons for acts" (Ormont, 2001, p. 286), and "modern group treatment employs a variety of techniques that realign the way members relate to each other" (Ormont, 2001, p. 78). I favor this approach to treatment, and here is why.

In the early days of training as a group therapist, I had read the work of Dr. Hyman Spotnitz, the founder of the Modern school. His most well-known treatise, commonly called "The Red Book" (Spotnitz, 1976) presented his hypothesis about the etiology of schizophrenia. Spotnitz believed that schizophrenics were mentally ill because as children they protected their parents, whom they simultaneously loved and hated, from aggression by turning their murderous impulses back onto themselves. This psychic event shattered their fragile egos, hence the development of psychotic symptoms. He called this process the *narcissistic defense*. His method of treatment was to foster the development of the negative transference and to encourage the patient's redirection of his or her hostile feelings onto the therapist (Spotnitz, 1976). This was a controversial idea, but it actually seemed to describe the difficult patients that I worked with; and my patients improved when I used his methods. Insight was of no use to a group member in such a regressed state.

The crux of working with difficult group members is the understanding of one's own countertransference, the induced feelings, metabolizing them and then constructively employing an intervention that furthers the group member's willingness and ability to talk about those emotions in the treatment. The mastery of techniques such as bridging, mirroring, joining, out-crazying, and confronting has helped me to learn my craft and to successfully run six weekly groups with difficult patients. The following is a case in point.

I had the experience of working with a family where unbridled aggression played a major role in the dysfunctional family dynamic. I have found that some of the techniques used in group therapy can be effective in family treatment as well, particularly when hostility is an issue. The family had initially contacted me for help with their adolescent son after he had been arrested for cyber-stalking, and group psychotherapy had been mandated by the court.

The teenager was the identified patient in the family, but it was my hypothesis that there was more to this than the boy's obstreperousness. As it turned out, both the parents enabled their son's bad behavior by failing to set limits for the boy. There were no consequences for his actions. Despite his arrest, the boy had unlimited access to the family computer.

The father was a successful professional man who ran his family as he ran his business. He was a bully and a tyrant, controlling the family by doling out money and then withholding it to punish family members who thwarted him. The mother, a bright but passive-aggressive woman, retaliated by complaining to her son about her unhappy marriage, and used him as a pawn in the ongoing war with her husband.

I believe that this put the son in the untenable position of being his mother's confidante, whom he both loved and needed but also resented for having been put in the middle. The boy's motives for cyber-stalking were multi-determined. I understood the behavior as threefold: 1) the boy's self-destructive attempt for attention, even if it were negative; 2) his acting out of his contempt for the father, and for authority in general; and 3) the acting out of his ambivalence toward his emotionally vacuous mother. Unable to contain the rage, he went into action.

After several months in group therapy, the young man, who was beginning to make some progress, abruptly decided to quit treatment when his court case was dropped. The night he told the group of his decision, one of the group members was incredulous: "I thought that *I* had anger issues!" The mother, rightly alarmed by this precipitous behavior, asked for a family session.

At the family session, the father told me that he had great respect for my profession but asked why, in the three months of group treatment, I had not stopped his son's two-pack-a-day smoking habit. When the word "but" is used in a sentence, the beginning part of the sentence is usually negated. He didn't have respect for my profession. Quite contrary to having respect for my profession, he held therapists in contempt. He wanted me to feel like a failure, as he must have felt about himself.

Rather than give him the opportunity to gratify his sadistic impulses toward me by asking him how I had failed his son, my intervention was to match his aggression with aggression: "Your son doesn't work. Where does he get the money to buy cigarettes?" The father replied: "I give him money to buy lunch, but he uses it to buy cigarettes." I said: "So you are part of the problem. Why not buy him a sandwich? Or better yet, bring home a half pound of baloney and white bread, and let him make his own sandwich."

The father became enraged. He stood up, and while throwing on his coat, he knocked over a lamp on the small table next to him, breaking the light bulb. As he was about to storm out of the room, I said, "Sit down and talk. You can leave when the session is over." He sat down and talked about his culpability for spending so many hours away from the family, and how he tried to assuage his guilty feelings by spoiling his son with money. As he left the session, he asked me how much he owed for the broken bulb. I told him thirty-five cents. He laughed, which meant to me that we had established a treatment alliance. This hypothesis was substantiated because the father has been more effective in setting limits for his son since that session. This indicates that there is often a connection between aggression and regression in group treatment. Regression is necessary for the treatment to progress, and aggression is an inevitable part of that process.

THE GROUP MEMBER'S PARADOX

In an earlier article (Pepper, 1996), I wrote that one of the most unequal of all adult social roles is that of patient in individual analytic psychotherapy. The imbalance is even greater in group treatment. Inequality exists in this professional therapeutic relationship between the leader and members for at least three reasons. First, the group is subordinate, deferring to the clinician's expertise and skill, and the member is also subordinate to the group's influence. The irony of this, of course, is that in reality the group members have the ultimate power—the simple fact is, that if no one shows up, there is no group. The group implicitly turns over control, allowing the leader to function as such.

Second, the healing process requires that the group member regress (Freud, 1921; Spotnitz, 1976). Paradoxically, the group and its members must allow the leader to control the treatment process in order for the regression to occur. Group process can then accelerate the regression process, more so than in individual treatment. The multiple transferences that develop can heat up the emotional atmosphere right from the start. The fact that members must share both time and space with each other makes for increased levels of frustration that are often rife with regressive transference material.

This leads directly to the third potential source of inequality in the professional treatment relationship: the clinician's own personality and its exploitive impact. Members are vulnerable to psychological mistreatment. The group must trust that the leader's motives are benign. And while mistakes are inevitable, the practitioner must be trustworthy, committed to the practice of his profession in an ethical manner. Anything less would constitute an abuse of power (Pepper, 1996). This trust is sometimes misplaced, however. For example, Dorpat (1985, 1996, 2006) describes the nefarious practices of some individual therapists who use their power to manipulate and control their patients.

The position of the patient entering treatment, group or individual therapy, is a paradoxical one. However, the paradox is not exactly the same for both. Patients usually enter individual treatment because they feel a measure of despair with the choices that they have made in their personal and/or professional lives, often seeking the clinician's attention and wanting relief from symptoms of anxiety and depression that these choices have produced. The competent and ethical individual clinician knows that his most legitimate function is to help the patient identify the emotions that underlie the choices and to provide the patient with an opportunity to make a conscious and deliberate decision whether to continue with life as it is or to make changes, in other words, to make the unconscious conscious.

In group therapy, the members enter treatment seeking relief from the emotional pain of dysfunctional relationships, often expecting the leader to help them to ameliorate their pain and to give them a quick fix. In analytic group therapy, the leader knows that his most legitimate role is to understand how the group and its members undermine their own efforts at improving the quality of their personal relationships. It is the clinician's responsibility to recognize the members' characterological obstacles that are blocking them from the achievement of greater emotional intimacy. This entails, in part, the leader's recognition of his or her own feelings of helplessness and inadequacy that often underlie the impulse to give advice and to make interpretations—neither of which is effective in resolving lifelong patterns of maladaptive behavior. The healing comes through the group process and the provision of corrective emotional experiences.

It is more than likely that in both instances, the prospective individual and group patients are, at best, only peripherally aware of the part that they have played in creating and maintaining their own emotional suffering. They don't usually realize that the therapy process can be painful. In fact, it is not linear, and there may be times when things may get worse before they get better. Patients may be unaware that, with proper titration, the experience of a modicum of emotional pain is ultimately in their best interest, and necessary for growth to occur.

This indicates that there is often a connection between aggression and regression in group treatment. Regression is necessary for the treatment to progress, and aggression is an inevitable part of that process.

THE REGRESSION—AGGRESSION CONNECTION

For example, I was the first member to arrive on time to my initial session of an ongoing group. When the others filed in, before any interactions took place, I was verbally attacked by a latecomer. She was furious that I was sitting in *her* seat. She demanded that I change seats. The leader reminded her that there was no assigned seating. His remark only further inflamed her.

After she calmed down, she revealed that she took an immediate dislike to me. I reminded her of her younger brother, whom her parents favored. It should be noted that the woman was herself a seasoned professional group therapist, an instance of the regressive power of group. To her credit, she stayed in the group and talked it through, thereby allowing the process to unfold.

The only legitimate function of the therapist is to help patients to understand the emotions that underlie their life decisions, as did the woman in the vignette above. It is up to the patient to do something about it. As we have seen, this is not always the case, as in altered treatment environments where the line between therapy and not-therapy is often blurred by the group therapist. This leads directly to a troubling thought: *What if the group therapist places his or her needs ahead of the patients'? Then what?* So here is another paradox.

If a patient comes to treatment because he has realized that his judgment is somewhat impaired, how can he trust himself to determine whether his choice of therapist is not another in a series of missteps in his life? If prospective patients choose a therapist using the same conflicted thinking that has determined past choices in relationships, then how are they to resolve their life's impasses? And if they can't trust their own judgment, relying on others to make life choices might only serve to further undermine their ego strength and sense of autonomy. In a recent *New York Times* article, David DeSteno puts it this way:

> Trust is a double-edged sword. Though you can accomplish more in life if you put your faith in others, doing so also leaves you vulnerable…But can you

> really trust yourself more than others? Recent findings suggest that the answer is no. (2014, p. 12)

DeSteno goes on to describe this dilemma from a cognitive theoretical framework saying that people are of two minds about everything; he assumes that human behavior is basically rational. I disagree. I believe that human behavior is ambivalent and largely unconscious. De Steno may have left out the most intriguing part of the story. That is, all of us have both healthy and neurotic needs and they are often in conflict. Sometimes the ambivalence is just below the surface. Our choices are dependent upon which set of needs is in ascendance at any point in time. How else can the seemingly inexplicable phenomenon of group therapists entering group treatment with their own "therapy" siblings be explained?

Robert Langs (1989) explicates it in his theory of the deep unconscious wisdom system.

Langs postulates that there are three levels of the mind: 1) the conscious mind, which manages cognitive thinking and rational decision making; 2) the deep unconscious memory system, which contains all painful remembrances from the past; and 3) the deep unconscious wisdom system, which is interested in emotional truth. According to Langs, these three systems are often in conflict because the conscious system tends to avoid the pain of emotional truth. As a consequence, decisions about relationships, including the choice of therapist, are often made on an irrational basis (Langs, 1989).

Langs argues that the conscious mind cannot be trusted to make lucid decisions in choosing a therapist, or in this case a group leader; and that, further, the deep wisdom system's perception of reality is not readily accessible, because those perceptions are often unpleasant and even painful and are therefore reflexively shunned. The unconscious wisdom system, Langs says, is revealed through encoded messages in dreams. He believes that the manner in which prospective patients select a therapist is a case in point.

While there are now internet websites where users can browse for a competent and an ethical clinician, selecting a therapist this way is going about it blindly. Langs believes that the most legitimate referrals come from professionals like medical doctors or other psychotherapists. Many believe that his position is too rigid and unrealistic but his point is clear. The manner in which a prospective patient knows the therapist, and what the patient knows about the therapist, will have an effect on the outcome of treatment (Langs, 1989).

This is equally true of group psychotherapy patients, albeit, once again, it is more complicated. *How group members know each other, what they know about each other, and how they know and what they know about the group leader all have a determining effect on the course of treatment and its outcome.* Our consumer-driven marketplace mentality has exacerbated the problem by creating therapist profiles that look more like dating websites, where headshots of therapists accompany a presentation of their personality characteristics, that have little or nothing to do with their competence as a therapist ("warm and caring" are not necessarily indicators of a therapist's expertise and skill). While this decision-making process may be challenging for prospective patients seeking individual psychotherapy, it is even more daunting for a prospective group member.

Members depend on the group, and the leader, to provide them with objective feedback as to how they come across in relationships. That is why members are in group in the first place. Implicit in group treatment is the trust, on the part of the member, that the group's perception of reality, by and large, is of greater validity than the perception of any one individual, themselves included. According to Goleman:

> A person alone is vulnerable to the sways of emotion or to blind spots arising from social prejudices, or to a failure to comprehend the complex consequences of a seemingly simple decision. . . . When they work at their best, groups can make better decisions than would any single member. (Goleman, 1985, p. 180)

But here's the thing: what if the group has a stake in denying aspects of reality, particularly as it relates to the personality and behavior of the leader? That is, what if the group colludes with the leader to protect him or her from close scrutiny? The dynamic process of mind control that Dorpat (1996) describes in individual therapy is even more pernicious in group.

In 1997 I wrote: "the art of psychotherapy is also a business. And with any business abuses exist. The old adage *Caveat emptor* applies to consumers of psychotherapy too" (Pepper, 1997, p. 215).

For instance, a woman psychotherapist joined a therapy group led by a grandiose and authoritarian leader who fashioned himself to be a Buddhist guru, a small roundish man with shaved head and a Fu-Manchu moustache. His treatment room was decorated like an Asian temple: a statue of a fat smiling Buddha, Chinese watercolors, and a bonsai tree. He climbed into a big swivel chair and sat shoeless in the lotus position. She thought: "This guy is cool; he fancies himself to be a guru dev." At the time, she longed for a strong, brilliant authority figure to counter the debilitating effects of having been raised by a sweet but weak and ineffectual father. She wanted a charismatic male group therapist. This was the early '70s. Her mantra was: "Anything goes," and here was a worldly, almost mystical, well-read, erudite, psychologically minded, funny, hip dude. She was hooked from the get-go. But something about the scene instinctively alarmed her. She was peripherally aware that his shoeless presentation was sexually provocative and overstimulating and made her feel uncomfortable, but she quickly pushed this awareness out of her mind.

During that first session, she decided that if he could take off his shoes, then so could she. But when she did, the group scolded her and told her that such behavior was an acting-in of her oppositional feelings toward authority. When she protested that she was only doing what the leader was doing, she was informed that it was different when he did it. When she asked why, the reply was simply, "That was the way it was." It seemed hard for her to believe that a group of apparently psychologically sophisticated people could be so passive and naïve. In the ensuing months, before she quit the group, she realized that the shoeless behavior and the group's passivity were representative of much larger boundary issues in that group (Pepper, 2014).

Sometime later, when she entered supervision with a clinician who had a clear sense of boundaries, she told him the story of the barefoot group leader. He was appalled at the group leader's penchant for working in his stocking feet. Her supervisor said that this was very inappropriate professional behavior and sarcastically quipped, "What other article of clothing was he planning to take off next?"

Even though this had registered with her during that first session, she didn't know what to make of it. She knew it meant something but not what. And perhaps, in and of itself, it was no big deal. But in light of other boundary issues that became apparent in the course of the treatment, this was a telltale sign.

Langs (1989), for example, notes this very same thing: "A part of something equals the whole…the example of a piece of clothing being equivalent to the person who wears it" (p.79). In my own work, I have come to understand that everything a therapist does and says reveals something about him, even his choice of office location and décor. It has to be that way and it isn't necessarily a bad thing either. But it means something; it always does.

In order for the frame to be secure, and for the transference to develop organically, i.e., from the patient's presentation of his life story, then the impact of the office location, décor, and the therapist's presentation of self, which is often referred to as *transparency*, should be kept to a minimum, not a big splash. For a long while, it should be all about the patient—otherwise it is too stimulating and actually interferes with the patient saying everything.

How then can group patients be protected from their own tendency to make treatment choices that are basically not in their best interests when their own judgment is impaired and they have to rely on the judgments of others whose judgments may be also impaired? The following incident comes from an article that I wrote, about this issue (Pepper, 1997).

At the time that it was written, I witnessed the substandard care that my supervisee's patient was receiving, at a clinic where I worked. The poor treatment was in part due to both a disturbing lack of boundaries between my supervisee and her patient and to insensitivity for frame maintenance that existed within the administration of the agency. The article was originally written from the perspective of an outside observer. In fact, I was the supervisor of the therapist in this occurrence and, although this case involves individual psychotherapy, there are implications for group therapy as well.

My supervisee, a neophyte staff therapist at the clinic, "Pat," in treatment with a teacher of hers at the institute that was affiliated with the clinic, agreed to treat a clinic patient who was a suicidal substance abuser and the son of one of the other staff therapists. Pat did not tell me about the case until after the treatment began. If she had, I would have strongly advised her not to take the case. I would have questioned the wisdom and ethics of the clinic's decision to accept the staff member's offspring as a patient in the first place. It wasn't until the patient's mother approached Pat to talk to her about the case that Pat brought the case to me; by then it was too late. The patient had made a serious suicide attempt and had to be hospitalized.

Listening to Pat's case presentation, I questioned her decision to accept this case and was concerned that the clinic director, in charge of patient assignments, allowed this arrangement. My concern was primarily for the patient but it was also somewhat self-serving—because as Pat's supervisor, I was accountable for the case. It was an untenable position. I had all the responsibility but no control over its disposition.

When this incident was initially published, I wrote that the clinic's acceptance of a staff member's son for treatment, at the very least, showed a lack of regard for appropriate boundaries; and while there was no way to know if the patient would have acted self-destructively had he been in a secure frame treatment milieu, receiving therapy at the clinic where his mother was on staff surely must have exacerbated the symptoms.

> Clearly, the patient's problems long preceded his entry into treatment; however, the obvious insensitivity of all parties to the clinical and ethical dangers of treatment under these circumstances could have only exacerbated his pathology. (Pepper, 1997, p. 218)

I wondered if Pat's choice of her own therapist, one of her institute teachers, was also indicative of a systemic lack of awareness of appropriate boundaries. Did Pat's therapist warn her of the potential danger of treating the offspring of a staff member? Pat didn't see it even when I pointed it out.

From the start, the patient may have had a hidden agenda. Pat's association to the clinic and to the mother contaminated the treatment even before it began. It was doomed to fail. In my clinical experience, I have found that when a patient enters treatment referred by someone for whom they harbor strong ambivalent feelings (whether the referral is from another professional or not), it is highly likely that the treatment will be unsuccessful. This is because the patient unconsciously wants to sabotage the treatment in an act of revenge toward the hated other. By undermining the treatment, the patient expresses his enormous aggression in a passive and self-destructive manner, thinking nothing of using himself as a weapon of his own demise.

The decision to seek treatment at the clinic where his mother was on staff was a poor one. But as noted above, a patient's choice of therapist is not always rational. In this instance, it was subversive and although the patient had some responsibility for the outcome of this case, I would argue that the choice is limited. The clinic and the therapist are ultimately responsible for deciding what is in the patient's best interest. Medical doctors are warned against treating relatives; it should be the same of therapists, even if the psychotherapist is only indirectly associated with the treatment.

There was a collective blind spot that included the clinic administration, the patient's mother, and my supervisee. Did greed play a role in the clinic's decision to accept this case? If the prime motive of any organization is to survive, in the age of diminished patient supply, then perhaps economic need compromised the clinic judgment.

I was subsequently informed that the clinic had allowed Pat to switch supervisors. Unlike private practice, where a supervisee employs a supervisor and can fire a consultant at will, the same latitude does not apply in a clinic or institute setting where the clinician is a student and, as a therapist, part of the staff. If a change is to take place there needs to be some type of formal process by which this occurs. When I confronted the clinic director, who signed off on this, she just shrugged her shoulders as if to say: "Sorry, it's a done deal." It was a *fait accompli.* This blind spot when it comes to boundaries in treatment applies to the practice of group therapy too. The forefathers of group psychotherapy suffered from it as well.

In a recent article (Pepper, 2013), I wrote that the seminal leaders of group psychotherapy have developed sophisticated theory and technique to resolve resistances to emotional intimacy (Ormont, 1974; Rosenthal, 1987; Spotnitz, 1976), treating conditions that Freud himself had thought impossible to treat (Freud, 1961). Countless numbers of group members have had their lives enhanced by their experience in treatment groups. It can truly be said that contemporary group therapists stand on the shoulders of giants.

While these clinical geniuses saw the world of interpersonal relations in a way that had not been envisioned before, they also suffered from at least one serious blind spot. Past leaders have largely overlooked the matter of boundaries. The frame of the treatment was not considered in the establishment of modern group psychotherapy. Further, the Modern school more than overlooks boundaries; it often disdains them, as exemplified in "The Analyst's Resolution of Revenge Resulting from the Treatment of his Parents" (E. Kramer, 1987) and "Marketing Psychotherapeutic Expertise" (Schumann, 2007), where the author unabashedly states, "A modern analytic suggestion is: Regard everyone as a potential client" (p. 84). One might ask: How do bright, psychologically minded, and basically ethical practitioners delude themselves into thinking that what they are doing is okay? In the article he was specifically referring to colleagues; but while reading Schumann's article I had a disturbing thought that seemed to follow logically from his suggestion. I wondered if the Modern Analytic community would be willing to consider the converse to that original suggestion, i.e., regard every client as a potential friend, lover, relative....

Gabbard & Lester studied boundary issues in individual psychotherapy, and concluded that boundary crossings are not inherently boundary violations (Gabbard& Lester, 1995, p. 123). Boundary violations occur only when patients experience negative treatment reactions that are directly related to the alterations of the frame. Group leaders who practice in small towns or in rural areas must deal with boundary crossings on a daily basis. Boundary crossings such as group member and therapist sharing the same gym, or running into each other at a public event like the opera, are inevitable and have meaning and engender feelings in both therapist and patient, but are incidental to the treatment and therefore are not the same order of experience as boundary violations, which are built into the structure of the relationship. Sometimes, the line between a boundary crossing and a boundary violation is not clearly delineated, and determinations of the propriety of an incident need to be examined on a case-by-case basis. The following episode is a case in point.

A colleague shared a harrowing experience in which a group member contacted her in the middle of the night begging for help. She had been raped and the rapist had threatened to kill her if she attempted to call 911. The member reached out to the group therapist out of her feelings of terror, pain, and anguish. The clinician felt obliged to go into action. Rather than calling the police on behalf of the patient, the clinician decided to go to the group member's home, escorted by her own husband, and personally take the patient to the hospital. In having done so, the group leader, as the first person to learn of the crime, became part of the subsequent legal proceedings.

While taking the group member to the hospital may have been a questionable decision, my colleague maintained that despite the ethical implications of breaching confidentiality, she believed that, under the circumstances, she had done the right thing. Afterward, the patient was able to express her gratitude and to talk about the incident in group. The long-term effects on the treatment of the clinician's involvement, however, were not clear.

It is possible that the patient's indebtedness and gratitude may have been too much for her to bear, thereby interfering with her willingness and ability to say everything. There may have been an unconscious resentment for having to contain any undesirable affect. After the incident, the group member became extremely dependent on the therapist. As a consequence, could it be that she was inhibited, thereafter, from verbalizing all of her negative feelings toward the group leader lest she appear unappreciative that her therapist had literally saved her life? In this case, however, the group patient was able to talk about the boundary crossing, albeit perhaps in a limited way. This is not usually the case when boundary violations occur.

The matter was further complicated by the clinician's reaction to the rape. Although this boundary crossing was incidental to the treatment, and not built into the fabric of their interactions as is the case with dual relationships, it still caused a serious psychological scar for the group leader.

The clinician suffered indirect trauma after she learned that the rapist had been apprehended; he had her name and phone number in his possession. She became a vicarious victim, "an occupational hazard," she said, for which she was not prepared. The leader became rightfully paranoid and had alarm systems installed in her home and at her office. Eventually, she moved out of state (personal communication to the writer).

One important difference between boundary crossings and boundary violations is that when boundary violations are enacted there is usually an unspoken directive from the leader to the patient not to talk about the transgression. To talk about the enactment would be to give it a reality that would pressure the leader into having to take responsibility for failing to contain strong destructive and self-destructive character flaws. As we shall see over and again, members tend to protect the leader from their serious foibles even under ideal conditions.

According to Gabbard & Lester (1995), in their study of non-sexual boundary violations in individual psychotherapy, such violations are the result of countertransference enactments. He states: "...it becomes clear that the concept has much in common with the Kleinian notion of projective identification" (Gabbard & Lester, 1995, p. 124). A similar idea presented by relational psychologists has been that of *therapist disclosure*. In fact, there has been a debate in the field that distinguishes between self-disclosure of emotion by the therapist and disclosure of self. Maroda (1999) clearly distinguishes between the individual therapist's timely and judicious use of feelings in the treatment and the revealing of personal facts about the therapist's personal life. This controversy applies to the field of analytic group psychotherapy as well, although the level of emotion may be greater. As Gans (1992) has noted in another context: "Unlike the comparable event in individual therapy, in group therapy the leader functions in a more intense and complicated emotional field" (p. 140). Gabbard does not study boundary violations in group, where their occurrence may be more than the result of idiosyncratic behavior.

The following vignette took place at a professional conference of group therapists. At this conference, I attended a workshop led by Dr. Leslie Rosenthal. The theme was "Preparing Groups for New Members." But before presenting this vignette, I would first like to add a backstory about my relationship with Dr. Rosenthal, in order to place this event in an appropriate context.

I first met Dr. Rosenthal at a previous workshop that he led. The theme was "Working with Difficult Groups." I was the only male participant in that group of about ten clinicians and had not known any of the women prior to the meeting. When I began to present a problem that I was having with a group of oppositional adolescents, a subgroup tried to turn the focus away from my problem with teens and put it back onto me.

They wanted to analyze my character flaws to determine how I created the group's negative reaction toward me. Dr. Rosenthal had to step in quickly. He said: "If this group's goal is to stop Dr. Pepper from presenting the case, you're doing a great job!" The subgroup backed off and I continued with the presentation.

He suggested that I encourage my adolescent group to continue finding fault with me. Dr. Rosenthal reasoned that, as oppositional teens, they would probably not do as I suggested. As it turned out, he was right. His suggestion to go with the flow worked. At the next meeting of the teen group, I invited them all to criticize me; they wouldn't do it. And the group moved on to talk about their conflicts with other authority figures. I called Dr. Rosenthal and thanked him both for helping me with my group and also protecting me in the workshop. I could understand why some colleagues referred to him as "The King of Joining" (Rosenthal, 1987).

Upon mulling over the dynamics of the workshop, it occurred to me that a parallel process had taken place. This group was acting like my adolescent group in its negative attitude toward me. I had come to the workshop seeking help with a group, and a subgroup wanted to change the level of the discussion to a personal one. The goal, under the guise of analysis, was to kill off the male member, I thought. This group, too, was oppositional. It wanted to change the purpose of the workshop from professional consultation to therapy, and pretty awful therapy at that. The point is that I liked Rosenthal and wanted to work further with him. I agreed with his thinking about how both of these two groups worked, but we diverged sharply when it came to boundaries.

Dr. Rosenthal began the workshop by presenting a cogent argument for the careful preparation of groups for the arrival of new members. If the group is not properly prepared for the newcomer, he reasoned, the new member may be bombarded with the members' feelings of infanticide and their displaced aggression away from the leader for bringing in the new member, resulting in the likelihood of the new member's premature termination from the group.

He took a dim view of greedy group therapists that, in a rush to fill their groups, place their own self-interest ahead of their patients' well-being. Dr. Rosenthal was righteously angry at those leaders whose narcissism motivated treatment decisions at their patients' expense. Clearly, this is a sound position for a group therapist to take. It would be impossible, however, for an outside observer to know that Rosenthal's own behavior belied his public stance.

I knew some therapists who were members of his treatment groups and who were socially involved with him and with each other, i.e., his patients were also his students, supervisees, and colleagues. And they in turn were socially involved with each other as fellow students, supervisees, colleagues, friends, and even relatives. In other words, he behaved unethically by establishing multiple-role relationships with his patients. As I previously noted, these relationships have been prohibited by professional organizations. And as I have also noted, the creation of multiple-role relationships is motivated partly by greed.

Unethical senior leaders often feed their practices on naïve neophytes who feel flattered to "sit at the master's feet." For Rosenthal to treat patients with whom he was socially involved would seem to confound his legitimate argument for the careful preparation of new patients. It seemed hypocritical; he took a self-righteous stand about greedy therapists and then appeared to be doing the same thing himself.

So I asked him a not-so-innocent question: "What are the effects of placing new patients in groups with people who are known to each other socially?" Rosenthal seemed amused by the question. He wasn't at all rattled when he turned to the others assembled in the room and chuckled, then said, "He's talking about incest!" I balked at asking the next most logical question: "So how long does it take to properly prepare a group for incest?"

"How could such a smart man have been so unaware?" I believe that there are several factors that may explain the blind spot. First, senior leaders who have been trained in a boundary-less environment tend to pass it along to the next generation of leaders. For this type of leader, blurred boundaries are ego-syntonic. As the senior leader said in Chapter 3, he was trained that way and so it was good enough for those that he taught. Second, because these leaders do not directly experience the negative effects of a compromised frame, they don't see that altering the frame of treatment always has consequences. Third, these leaders often believe that they are so well trained and psychologically sophisticated that the rules of treatment do not apply to them. This is their conceit. They can engage in taboo relationships without suffering the consequences. Unfortunately, it is the group and its members who do.

When boundaries are blurred in group therapy, two things happen. First, the leader's directive to say everything is obviated by the treatment itself. The leader's interference with the contract actually subverts group members' willingness and ability to say everything; hence the second thing happens—a conspiracy of silence ensues. No one talks about the contaminated treatment.

In the next chapter, the seven dangers of blurred boundaries will be presented. Dangers exist because they do harm. When members are in a double-bind, saying everything becomes unwise, not the politic thing to do, or worse, iatrogenic treatment reactions may occur. This reality applies to all members in a blurred boundary setting, including group therapists themselves in treatment in a compromised milieu.

Chapter Five

The Seven Dangers of Blurred Boundaries in Group Therapy

It never ceases to amaze me when I witness, hear about, or read accounts of bright, experienced, psychologically sophisticated group leaders who do not see how the blurring of boundaries between therapy and not-therapy compromise the treatment. Ethical clinicians, as well as unethical ones, both suffer this blind spot, as we have seen and shall continue to see over and again.

Michael Lewis, writing in another context, where he tries to make sense of the factors that cause panic in the stock market, said: "You cannot really see a thing unless you know what you are looking for" (Lewis, 2009, p.126). This applies to the subject of blurred boundaries in group therapy as well. Take the matter of confidentiality and gossip in group. In an article about gossiping in group psychotherapy, Gans (2014) notes:

> Gossip would appear to be the opposite of what takes place in a therapy group. . . . Therapy groups, with their boundary and confidentiality agreements, seek to create feelings of safety and trust. . .gossip, especially malicious gossip, creates mistrust, violates boundaries, harms reputations, and avoids person-to-person exchange. (p. 7)

After having said this, he simply drops a discussion of the connection between blurred boundaries, gossip, and negative treatment reactions. In fact, there is only one paragraph in the article that is devoted to the subject of gossip and boundary violations.

In a secure frame environment, gossiping cannot really occur. Since members are anonymous to each other outside the group, and there isn't any social contact, no real-life harm can come to members if the group talks about them behind their back.

It is a different story if members have dual relationships with each other in which case outside the group gossiping can have serious consequences, and is in fact, a violation of confidentiality. Although he doesn't attend to it, there *is* a vignette in Gans's article that looks to me like a place where this may have occurred. I'll have more to say about it a bit later in this chapter. But for now, let's take a step back and look at the bigger picture of confidentiality in analytic group therapy.

1. BREACHES OF CONFIDENTIALITY

In a previous article, I wrote:

> One of the basic principles for the practice of ethical analytic group psychotherapy is confidentiality. Most group practitioners would agree that this is a cornerstone of the work. In fact, the Code of Ethics for the American Group Psychotherapy Association includes a section on confidentiality (AGPA, 1999). Without the assurance of complete privacy, and that all participants agree that nothing leaves the room, then security for the frame of treatment could not exist. (Pepper, 2004a, p. 103)

As Philips (2013) has noted, confidentiality like autonomy is never absolute, even in a secure-frame environment. My own experience supports this observation.

For example, one night a woman in one of my groups spoke about a job interview that she had at a prestigious firm. A male group member, with a long history of fluid ego boundaries, who also happened to be looking for a job, coincidentally at the same firm, turned to her at the next group meeting and told her that her name had come up during the week. Shocked, she asked what he was talking about. He said that in his own job search he had spoken with a recruiter at that firm and mentioned that a friend of his had recently interviewed there. Since he didn't know her last name, he used her first name and the position that she was applying for. The recruiter recognized the description and said: "Oh, you mean...." and then said her full name.

She was furious with him for violating confidentiality and she turned to me and threatened: "I no longer feel safe here...and if you don't remove him from the group, I'm leaving." While I acknowledged her right to feel angry about his breach of privacy, I asked her why her reaction was so extreme. Her response was somewhat paranoid. She feared that she would not get the job if the recruiter associated her with this other member, whom she disdained and thought was "a loser."

He was defensive and incredulous. He was not at all able to take her reaction seriously and maintained that he hadn't done anything wrong. He said that anyone in the similar situation would have done the same. He thought he was right and she was wrong. Here again was a case of a fellow who had no idea how he came across in relationships. He was unable or unwilling to look at his part. Had he allowed it, the group could have helped him with this insensitivity to the feelings of others.

This bullheaded position reflected the very same attitude that got him into trouble in his real-life relationships; I supported his honesty in telling the group the truth. My support fell on deaf ears, however; he didn't see the damage he had done to his own credibility in the group and how it related to his difficulties in his personal life. I told him that if he believed that the key to successful relationships was to determine who was right and who was wrong in any conflict, then he was doomed to a rather bumpy ride in life. The whole thing was no big deal to him. He didn't get it. Even though he was aware of the rule that everything that goes on in the room stays in the room, he didn't understand why it was important. And he is not alone in this. Many group members do not abide by the rule of group privacy even if the need for it is explained to them, but it is not only some group members who don't see the point. There are those who should know better but don't.

On one occasion, I received a call from a representative of a nascent training institute established around the teachings of a brilliant, charismatic leader. At that time, I was a student of his in a private training group. The institute was sponsoring a fund-raising drive and was soliciting money from anyone associated with the leader. I asked how they got my name. The caller said that she had been given a list of potential donors, derived in part from the leader's practice. Then it got even worse. I listened in amazement as she told me that the amount donated would determine how my name would appear in the institute's fund-raising drive journal: student contributor, donor, sponsor, and benefactor! *This contact list contained the names and phone numbers of the leader's patients and students!*

This was a flagrant violation of confidentiality and I told the leader so at the next group meeting. But he didn't get it. His defense was that since he didn't personally make the calls then no harm had been done. The thorny issue of confidentiality can even be a confusing one to grasp for professional psychotherapists who write about their clinical experiences. The following is from a short article that I wrote on the subject (Pepper, 2014b).

> As an author of articles on boundaries, I have often fretted (along with other writers on psychotherapy) over the challenge of using clinical material while protecting confidentiality of the patients. Some of us have met this task with mixed results.
>
> Returning to the work of George Weinberg (1993), in *Nearer to the Heart's Desire*, a collection of case vignettes, he writes in the preface that "All names, physical descriptions, places, times of occurrence and identifiable events have been changed". (Weinberg,1993, p. vii).

> However, in the chapter entitled "Tennis, Anyone?", the story of a troubled female professional tennis player, Weinberg disguises her identity only to provide the reader with the real names of other women that she played with and against, obviously revealing his patient's identity to anyone knowledgeable about tennis, or inclined to look up the matches in which she played!
> As complicated as it is writing about individual psychotherapy patients, it is even more complicated when writing about group therapy. The ethical writer disguises identities, but sometimes members recognize themselves anyway, as Stone (2014) also points out. And even if the injury doesn't rise to the level of an ethical violation, damage can be done.
> In one case from my own writing, a middle-aged female group member was able to identify herself in an article that I had published about boundaries. She told me in front of the other members that she felt angry, hurt, and betrayed by me. The group rallied around her, supported, and protected her. Even though I had been scrupulous in hiding critical identifying facts, she figured out whom I was talking about. And just when I thought it all might turn into a group revolt, she said something that shifted the whole mood in the room.
> She told the group that what had offended her most was that I had referred to her in the article as "middle-aged." The group erupted in hilarious laughter. We moved on, and she moved on.
> In retrospect, one factor that seemed to have played a significant role in defusing the potential for greater harm here was that the group took place in a secure-frame environment. There was no contact outside the group. I believe that anonymity and safety were preserved; looping could not occur. No part of it could come back to haunt her in her real life.
> Both examples have at least one thing in common; they both reflect, to some extent, the author's acting out of countertransferential feelings toward the patients in question. Stone's final reminder seems apt here: "If you wish to present clinical material, you will be well served to explain the purpose of your presentation" (Stone, 2014, p.154).
> Could it be that Weinberg's decision to disclose the identities of his patient's famous colleagues was an act of self-aggrandizement? Who knows? As for me, I may have put angry feelings into play by writing about having felt intruded upon. Has the integrity of our presentations been compromised as a result? (Pepper, 2014b).

In general, there may be several reasons why some people cannot maintain confidentiality. First, there is secondary-gain gratification derived from gossiping, as Gans reports: "One motive in social comparison is the maintenance of self-esteem" (Gans, 2014, p. 8). People may simply like to talk about the *mishegoss* (craziness) of others. This may be done, perhaps, in an effort to place their own troubles into perspective, allowing them to feel comparatively normal. As a result, group members do not always understand the necessity of complete privacy of meetings. Second, there may be a tendency to confuse talking outside of group about the feelings and issues churned up, without necessarily revealing the details of the sessions and the identities of members. Consequently, there can be a lack of awareness of the potential untoward impact of this seepage on the treatment. The intensity of group meetings may be too much for some members to contain and so leakage occurs. While the ability to maintain appropriate boundaries is a complicated, and perhaps a lifelong one to master, the clinical consequences of a lack of confidentiality are immediately apparent. At the very least, talking about group outside the treatment dilutes its power. For this reason, many analytically oriented group therapists have a rule that prohibits any outside social contact (Pepper, 2004a).

The intrusion of managed health care, however, has added a major complication to the matter of patient privacy in *all* treatment modalities (see Giles, 1993). Yet, even without third-party interference, the issue of confidentiality is quite complex in a group treatment setting. The very nature of group, with the sheer number of participants and all the possible permutations and combinations for boundary crossings, virtually insures the inevitability of violations of privacy.

This is not to suggest that all group therapists deliberately mislead members when informing them about the rules about confidentiality. As ethical practitioners, most do not want the group experience to harm participants. There is no way, however, that a leader can protect the complete secrecy of group meetings. In fact, there may be circumstances in which protection is not warranted. In one famous case, a man attending an AA meeting was arrested when a group member reported him to the authorities after he had shared in the group that he had killed someone.

Still, even under less dramatic circumstances, total privacy is not assured in group. While full anonymity is an ideal to which members and leaders may aspire, it is seldom attained. Some professional organizations recognize this fact and refer to it in their code of ethics. For example, the Clinical Social Work Federation's code of ethics states: "Clinical social workers treating couples, families and groups seek agreement among the parties involved regarding each individual's right to confidentiality…clients involved in this type of treatment should, however, be informed that the clinical social worker cannot guarantee that all participants will honor their agreement to maintain confidentiality" (Clinical Social Work Federation, 1997, p. 8).

Just as parents cannot save their children from all the dangers of the world, group therapists are limited in their ability to shield members from all untoward occurrences in group, including violations of confidentiality. Group leaders need to acknowledge this reality to prospective members during the screening interview. For instance, when I offered a patient the opportunity to join one of my treatment groups, he expressed doubts. He said that previously he had been in a group where members violated each other's privacy. As a result, he was reluctant to participate in group therapy again. I told him that his concern was a valid one and that a totally sheltered environment could not be guaranteed with 100 percent certainty (Pepper, 2004a).

There may be some treatment situations in which confidentiality is virtually impossible to keep, even if all participants agree in principle to maintain it. This can occur when blurred boundaries are built into the system. Under certain conditions, breaches of privacy are an intrinsic part of the social fabric of the group, as in the case of inpatient psychotherapy groups, groups run in small towns, or in many group training institutes across the country where dual relationships exist and where looping, another danger to be discussed next, may occur. At times, the peril of breaches of confidentiality can reach outrageous proportions where the member's right to privacy is all but obliterated.

A colleague asked my opinion on a predicament that she was in. Her group supervisor put my colleague's own patient, also a practicing group leader, into the same supervision group that she was in. Understandably, she felt very uncomfortable about the prospect of sharing personal information in front of her own patient. However, my colleague admitted that she was so financially dependent upon the leader, who was her source of referrals, that she colluded with the leader against herself and stayed in this crazy arrangement. She had finally had enough when she began to experience anxiety and depression every time she went to group and wanted to leave it but feared that in doing so she would "burn her bridges." She was apprehensive about alienating the "mother—feeder" and losing the leader's approbation. She wanted to know what I thought she should do. I asked her if she were so desperate for referrals that she would be willing to trade her mental health, and that of her patient, for money and stay in this exploitative, but financially lucrative relationship. She left the group soon thereafter (Pepper, 2014a).

My colleague's discomfort and anxiety were directly related to the behavior of the group supervisor, who put my colleague in the untenable position of having a social relationship with her own patient. For her part, my colleague's own neediness had compromised her good judgment and she stayed until she couldn't take it anymore.

For the leader's part, his sense of omnipotence, that he could bend the rules without any consequence, and his greed to feed his own supervisory practice combined to blind him from seeing that he had created an emotionally incestuous relationship between my colleague and her patient, while simultaneously creating a pathologically dependent and an emotionally abusive relationship between my colleague and himself.

I have come to the ironic conclusion that the lack of confidentiality in the group leaders' own treatment and training may be the most compromised treatment of all! (2014). The following vignette was first published from the perspective of a third-person observer (Pepper, 2004a).

I was in a supervision group with a well-known group leader. On one occasion, I complained in group about my individual supervisor, who had been excessively harsh and critical of my handling of a case. The senior leader proceeded to tell me in front of the entire group that he knew my individual supervisor and had had a professional relationship with him. The leader went on to say that my individual supervisor was actually his (the senior leader's) patient in a therapy group. The senior leader explained that the offending supervisor was actually making progress resolving his issues with narcissism. Although we sat in stunned silence after this egregious breach of confidentiality, nothing was said and the group moved on to another presenter.

2. LOOPING

This is similar to a breach of confidentiality, in which private information shared in one context is inappropriately revealed in another. Breaches of confidentiality can occur without looping but looping does not occur without a breach of confidentiality. This often happens when group members are in dual relationships with each other.

Goffman (1961) first described this phenomenon in *Asylums*, his famous study of the social structure of total institutions like prisons, the military, and mental hospitals. One part of his work focused on the dynamics of inpatient psychotherapy groups. He observed that looping occurs when patients' confidential information that they present in treatment groups gets fed back to them in other social contexts. There was no segregation of action for inpatients; behavior in any interaction was available to staff and other to inpatients to be referred back to in other dealings. Since the boundaries were so blurred in the hospital, inpatients had to learn to reveal only information about themselves that would not rebound and harm them in other hospital settings.

Yalom (1985) once said that he learned through experience that the two most important goals of long-term group psychotherapy—symptom relief and character change—must be modified within the structure of an inpatient unit. While he believed inpatient groups can be therapeutic, their aims must necessarily be more modest due, in part, to the blurred boundaries in that environment (Pepper, 2007). My own experience supports this observation.

As a neophyte group therapist, I ran groups in upstate New York prisons. One group was at the Bedford Hills Correctional Facility for Women in Katonah. The group consisted of eight to ten prisoners who had been incarcerated for a variety of felonies, like drug dealing, embezzlement, and even murder. I had been informed of this before starting the group but was not told which prisoners committed which crimes; further I was told not to ask them why they were in jail. I knew that one of the women had murdered her children in a Medea-like attempt at protecting them from her estranged husband, who threatened to take them.

For the first several sessions, there was very little talking and the atmosphere was extremely tense. Although we all, save one, sat in a circle, no one wanted to talk about herself, which was completely understandable under the circumstances. "Was there privacy in prison?" they wanted to know. I couldn't assure them that there would be.

What little talking there was centered on the rules. Were they allowed to smoke? Could they take bathroom breaks? The armed guard at the door reminded me that the rules were not mine to make. I decided that I would leave the room during a cigarette break. But even my attempts to get them to talk about why they didn't want to talk failed to move the group along.

Though groups, in general, are often reluctant to speak, it was more complicated here because no one could be sure if what was said would stay in the room. Looping was clearly a potential danger in prison. I realized very quickly that I would have to adjust my thoughts as to how the group would run. I decided that we should discuss books about interpersonal relationships as a way of engaging them in conversation about feelings without their necessarily having to reveal anything personal. The prison had funds to purchase paperbacks. So between meetings they read, and we discussed the readings and slowly some personal material emerged. Throughout the weeks that the group ran, however, the one who sat outside the circle never spoke. She sat off in a corner, silently crocheting baby booties. The group was tolerant of her ambivalent attitude toward the meetings. She wanted to be present but she didn't want to participate. For my part, I couldn't help but wonder if *she* were the one. Nowadays, with the advent of managed health care, matters of privacy are complicated for most groups even outside of prison. Looping and breaches of confidentiality are often closely linked, as the following example reveals. This seems prevalent in the world of group therapy training.

Breaches of Confidentiality and Looping in Professional Settings

At some analytic group training institutes, a Mad Hatter's tea party–like atmosphere seems to permeate interactions both within the treatment groups and outside of them. A conspiracy of denial exists within these institutes. Participants do not acknowledge the existence of a contradiction between their belief about confidentiality at the institute and reality.

A colleague, "Suzy," responded to a listserv request that I posted asking group therapists if they would share their experiences in dual relationships. Suzy reported that she had enrolled at a group therapy institute that was headed by "Joannie," her own women's group therapy leader. In other words, her group therapist became her boss. After years of treatment, Suzy decided that she wanted to join a group that was coed, to work on her issues with men. She discussed her plans with the leader and the group and went through a termination process, then joined a group led by a male therapist, a man who was not affiliated with the training institute.

Soon thereafter her advisor at the institute contacted Suzy to say that she had heard that Suzy was no longer in treatment with Joannie. The advisor also knew that Suzy was now in treatment with a man who was not affiliated with the institute. Suzy was stunned and felt betrayed that her confidentiality had been breached. She asked her advisor how she knew all this, to which the advisor replied ominously, "I make it my business to know such things."

Adding insult to injury, the advisor then told Suzy that since the male therapist was not part of the organization, her time spent in treatment with him could not be counted to fulfill the institute requirement for group treatment hours needed for graduation. Suzy left the meeting in a daze. She was furious, hurt, and incredulous. *How could this have happened?* she thought. She was also angry with herself for having been so naïve as to have trusted these people. She questioned the integrity of her director/therapist and her own judgment for having been in treatment with her in the first place.

If this sordid episode weren't egregious enough, the injury was compounded at an institute social function when a casual acquaintance approached her and said, "I heard you left your therapist for a man!" My colleague was stunned and was beside herself with rage.

The most troubling aspect of this incident was that, until she and I spoke, Suzy blamed herself for having participated in this mess. Instead of using this event as a learning experience, she used it to denigrate herself. Suzy was self-critical and now, in retrospect, thought that she should have known better than to join her own therapist's organization. Prior to our conversation, she had begun to doubt herself, minimizing the effect of this incident on her. She had worried that she was making a bigger deal about this than it was.

I reassured Suzy that her feelings of betrayal over these breaches of confidentiality were valid. Although Suzy did bear some responsibility for having placed herself in a compromised treatment environment, and hence there was an element of truth to her having been naïve to think that her privacy would be respected in this boundary-less milieu, this was certainly not entirely her problem. In fact, I told her that she had been traumatized. Suzy had every right to feel rage. She *had* been betrayed and she had been looped as well. To disallow treatment hours with the unaffiliated male leader could be seen as punishment for having left treatment with Joannie. How could the advisor have known about Suzy's new therapy without someone violating her privacy? Suzy felt troubled by all this. She told me that she has been revisiting the occurrence periodically over the years and struggled to reconcile her belief that privacy was a high priority at the institute, when in reality it was not.

Since then, Suzy has been reluctant to participate in group therapy, despite the fact that she is a practicing group therapist. Clearly, damage had been done to her. How many other clinicians have similar stories to tell but who have kept their experience of iatrogenic treatment reactions to themselves? This is the conspiracy of silence.

I, too, have struggled with the prospect of being looped in group therapy (Pepper, 2013). In the following case, both of us wore two hats. Apparently, the existence of the rule of confidentiality and the adherence to it within the profession are two separate things.

I had worked as a staff therapist at a clinic that was affiliated with a training institute and I simultaneously was in group therapy, in a group run by a clinic director. I became interested in working as a supervisor at that clinic. In order to be considered for the position, I agreed to be interviewed by a clinic administrator who was simultaneously one of my own group therapy siblings. The purpose of the meeting was so that the sibling/administrator could determine my fitness for the supervisory position.

At the time, I was experiencing a real-life personal crisis, suffering an emotional breakdown in the form of an agitated depression as a result of the death of my father and the loss of a failing marriage. I was anxious and worried about the prospect of being interviewed by someone who had quite intimate knowledge of my disturbed emotional state and had the power to use that knowledge, from his position of authority, to deny me the position that I sought. I felt paranoid about the prospect of my group therapist/clinic director and my group sibling/clinic administrator conferring about me behind my back. It was clear that my paranoia and anxiety about the interview were related, at least in part, to the compromised and incestuous relationship that I had with both the clinic director and my group sibling at the clinic. I feared that confidential information would be looped back to harm me.

3. GASLIGHTING

As I have noted in an earlier paper (Pepper, 1997), the art of psychotherapy is also a business, and with any business abuses exist. The art of group psychotherapy is no exception. Among the issues that can lead to group member abuse is that of whose needs come first—the leader's or the group's?

Observers of the practice of individual psychotherapy have described a fascinating defense employed by some therapists who protect their own emotional stability at the expense of their patients. *Gaslighting*, as it is known, refers to an unconscious process whereby the therapist invalidates a patient's perception of reality and thereby undermines the patient's emotional strength (Dorpat, 1985,1996, 2006; Calef & Weinshel, 1981).

In the movie, *Gaslight,* the story unfolds in turn-of-the-century London where the homes are lit by gas, hence the title. Each night when the husband goes out, the lights mysteriously dim. When his wife asks him to confirm her perception, he tells her that she is imagining things. Through a series of related events, the wife comes to question her own sanity. The husband, who has separated her from all outside social contact, becomes her sole source of substantiation. The motive for his insidious scheme is greed. The husband wants her out of the way, in a mental hospital, so that he can claim sole possession of her large inheritance. She is saved from being driven completely mad by a handsome stranger who has been witnessing her slow deterioration from a distance and steps in just in the nick of time to show her that her perceptions of the husband's nefarious plan for her are valid.

At the end of the movie, the wife is spared being driven crazy. She is saved by someone who provides her with the opportunity to talk about her experience and to observe the pattern of her husband's behavior. Once her perception of reality had been validated, she then had the emotional strength to break free of his control.

In an analogous way, perhaps, when a patient in individual treatment is gaslighted by their therapist, then a consultation with someone other than the therapist can help to resolve a treatment impasse. Dorpat (2006) has noted that sometimes patients do not realize they have been gaslighted until they enter treatment with someone who treats them differently. While this may also apply to gaslighting in group, the dynamics are not quite the same. In fact, the matter is generally more complicated.

The danger in group is twofold: 1) that the member's negative reaction gets interpreted as transference, a distorted view of reality based on his or her history, when in fact it is not distortion at all but a realistic response to a contaminated treatment environment (such as the case of Sonny in Chapter 2, who was told that his symptoms of anxiety and depression were related to his conflicted relationship with his father rather than because his group leader was using him as a servant or the woman whose jealousy over being excluded from the leader's inner circle was interpreted as sibling rivalry from her family of origin transferred to the present, or the woman who demurred sharing personal information with others in group that she knew socially but was told that her reluctance was an indication of her inability to be emotionally intimate); 2) there is a double-whammy effect to gaslighting in group that doesn't exist in individual psychotherapy because the shared culture of members, which protects the leader from close scrutiny, coupled with the leader's power derived by virtue of the role, skews the perception of reality toward the leader's view, leaving the gaslighted member without validation of his or her view. This is crazy-making.

While the villainous plan concocted by the husband in the movie was conscious and deliberate, the gaslighting that occurs in psychotherapy groups may not be. Nonetheless, the underlying motive of greed may be the driving force in both instances, with the same potential for disaster.

The question of whose needs come first poses a moral dilemma for many individual therapists, but the dilemma is thornier in group, where the leader's character is on display in front of an audience.

Many view their profession as a calling rather than as a vocation. There are some who recoil at the thought of psychotherapy as a business. Their guilt influences their perception of working for money. Some have actually said that psychotherapists should not get rich as a result of their practice and have set their fees accordingly. They believe that doing otherwise is exploitative and potentially abusive. However, there may be confusion as to the difference between taking care of oneself in money matters and greed (Pepper, 2001b). The fact that many practitioners accept the cultural belief that mental health workers shouldn't be avaricious reflects the profession's conflict. Since the general public and some group leaders assume that mental health-care practitioners should aspire to a high moral calling, many wrestle with the impulse to act on feelings of oral greed in the treatment. *We should be above it all.* The cultural myth of the warm, caring, and selfless clinician runs counter to any notion of the therapist as a greedy businessperson.

The issue of whose needs come first in treatment applies to more than money. It also relates to other treatment frame issues. It is my impression that group leaders who unconsciously make frame-of-treatment decisions such as setting and raising fees, overfilling groups with too many members, tacitly or blatantly discouraging terminations after many years of treatment, engaging in dual relationships with group members, and making referrals to practitioners who are simultaneously their group patients on the basis of greed, may be doing harm to their groups (Pepper, 2001b). This harm may come in the form of gaslighting.

In his article entitled, "Group Dynamics," Elliot Schumann states: "The objectives of group psychotherapy are awareness of 'what is going on'" (Schumann, 1999, p.24). Schumann describes how the leader facilitates the choice of preferable alternative behavior by transforming communications from the unspoken to the spoken. Assumedly, the clinician's motives are benign. But as I pointed out in Chapter 3, this assumption isn't always valid. In fact, there are circumstances where the leader's unconscious motive is to obfuscate what is really going on and to exploit the group's dependency on her or him. Further, the group may be used as an unwitting coconspirator in undermining a member's (or the entire group's) accurate perception of reality, in an effort to foster an environment in which the leader's greed and narcissism are gratified as the expense of others.

Writers on the subject of gaslighting in individual psychotherapy such as Dorpat (1985) and Calef and Weinshel (1981) were the first to connect the storyline of *Gaslight* with the unconsciously driven behavior of some therapists. They describe how the wish to incorporate the object can lead some clinicians to undermine their patients' perceptions of reality. These practitioners unwittingly jeopardize their patients' treatment, and hence psychological well-being in order to control the interactional environment (Calef & Weinsel, 1981).

In his book *Defense and Denial in the Psychotherapy Situation,* Dorpat (1985) describes how the clinician's greed is unconsciously denied. The patient's accurate perception of the clinician is disavowed so as to avoid the emotional experience associated with the acting out of the therapist's oral hunger (Dorpat,1985). The gaslighting that occurs in group therapy can be magnified in its toxicity by a phenomenon that I will address more fully in the section called the emperor's new clothes effect. Since a group, by definition, consists of more than two members, there is the added dimension of a group culture, a shared reality that obviously doesn't exist in individual psychotherapy.

Here is another paradox: *The group culture gives this modality its power, on the one hand, and its potential for harm, on the other.* While in the grip of a shared group reality, it is virtually impossible for a member to sustain an alternative, conflicting, and negative view of what is going on in a compromised group environment. Like the wife in the movie, there needs to be an outside source of perceptual validation, one that is highly cathected (where there is a strong emotional attachment), to break the hold of a gaslighted treatment environment. The next vignette is a case in point, and is one that I personally witnessed.

Vignette: Melvin's Story

One day, the leader of a training group in which I was a member presented a problem that she was having with one of the group members. She wanted the group's advice on how to handle the situation. Here's some background information about this episode. Melvin, an experienced group therapist, had approached the group leader with a business deal. Melvin wanted to co-author a book. The leader agreed, but when the book was published Melvin's name appeared first under the title. The leader was furious and asked the group for help.

She told us that she was having a countertransference reaction to Melvin and it was interfering with her work with him as his supervisor and group therapist. The leader said that she was in a rage toward Melvin and felt betrayed. She told the group that Melvin's competitive feelings toward his parents had infiltrated the treatment process. Tearfully, Melvin responded by saying that he loved her as a therapist but he hated her persona. He felt terribly hurt that the leader could be so cold. In his mind, this was a misunderstanding on the part of the publisher. A group member, Jojo, was furious that the leader had breached Melvin's confidentiality by revealing his status as a patient.

I was asked my opinion. I said that the writing of a book could be seen as a symbolic creation of a child and that the leader and Melvin had made a "love child" together. In blurring the boundaries, the transference and countertransference had become hopelessly contaminated. For the leader to interpret Melvin's behavior as an acting out of competitive feelings toward his parents was gaslighting. The leader had taken control of reality by labeling Melvin's behavior transference. At the same time, Melvin could not risk feeling anger toward the leader lest she reject him and withhold the unconscious gratification that was built into their relationship. Melvin had bested all other competitors by being so close to her. For her part, the leader had lost the right to interpret Melvin's behavior as transference. He had seen too much of her nether side for his reaction to be purely distortion.

It may seem unfathomable to the layman that professional group therapists could create and remain in such contaminated treatment environments. Clearly, a collective blind spot existed in that group. The leader's narcissism and self-interest were preserved at the cost of awareness and perhaps the emotional stability of group members. This is also an example of the Emperor's New Clothes effect in group. The group and the leader unconsciously agree to avoid the obvious reality. One might wonder what otherwise bright and perceptive people get out of not seeing what is right in front of them (Pepper, 2014).

It is my impression that group therapists, as group patients themselves, are no different from other group patients. Consequently, they experience the same regressive forces in treatment. The unconscious wish to be cared for by the group leader and to be a part of his therapy "family" exists independently of education, training, and psychological sophistication. However, in a boundary-less environment the line between reality and distortion can become blurred. Since the leader allows treatment decisions to be made on the basis of narcissistic gratification, then the impulse toward unconscious gratification can be strong for the patient/therapists as well, so strong in fact that they may be all too willing to overlook behavior on the senior leader's part that is foolish, treatment destructive, or worse.

As with emotional incest, this constitutes an abuse of power. R. D. Laing (1970) has noted that the fastest way to drive someone crazy is to deny his or her view of reality. The group leader cannot always be trusted to represent the group's best interest. It may be necessary for someone outside the system to provide it, although it does not have to be a stranger, as was the case in the movie.

An organic and authentic resolution to the problem of what Slater (1974) has called "inner circuitry" thinking is through group process. Just as the leader of a group resolves a group resistance by identifying it, studying its function, and talking about it, similarly the profession of group therapists can resolve the resistance to understand the phenomenon of gaslighting. This is the very same operation the profession can perform. Professional organizations like the American Group Psychotherapy Association and the American Psychological Association can include workshops and sponsor conferences on the effects of gaslighting, greed, and dual relationships in group psychotherapy, and in this way raise the consciousness of practitioners. This would help to alert the professional community to its potential harm.

It should be noted, however, that the resistance to change can be quite formidable. The investment in the status quo is so strong that even those group members who are directly affected by gaslighting are reluctant to modify their own behavior. For example, several years ago a colleague and friend of mine joined a group where the members were socially involved with her and with each other. Within a few sessions, she became irritated with the lack of vitality in the group. Sometimes in these incestuous groups, where members are in dual relationships with each other, there is a quality of deadness that is related to members' unwillingness to engender negative feelings toward themselves, other members, or the leader. As noted earlier, under these conditions members are reluctant to make waves and thereby jeopardize their positions in the system.

Not long thereafter, I told my friend that I had been invited to present a paper on the topic of dual relationships in group psychotherapy at a professional conference. It was unsettling when she asked me, "What are dual relationships?" Since we had had a recent discussion about the iatrogenic treatment reactions to dual relationships, I wondered to myself how this bright, perceptive, successful professional could have forgotten all that we talked about over the last few months. The answer was obvious but a bit disconcerting—she simply didn't want to take it in. It was too threatening to consider, and so it was all denied. This is a chilling example of the extent to which a group member will go to avoid experiencing the anxiety attendant to the separation from a system that she, herself, had identified as toxic.

However, there can be a positive side to all this, as the next vignette reveals. In fact a group can serve as an *anti-gaslighting* agent. It occurred in a group that I ran where I almost "gaslighted" a group member.

There was a woman in that group who reminded me of a former girlfriend. They looked quite similar and came from the same ethnic and religious background; and both had a history of ambivalent feelings about romantic relationships, pushing and pulling men in and out of their lives.

After the relationship with my girlfriend ended badly, I began taking out my frustrations on my patient in group. Technically speaking, I was displacing negative feelings onto her. I was openly critical of the choices of men whom she dated, made sarcastic comments about her habitually coming late to group, picked on her when I thought she wasn't active enough in group.

One night I made what I thought was a brilliant interpretation, and told her that she confused a man's strength with his sadism. She said that she had

had enough of my belligerence and proceeded to read me the riot act. She said that she was sick and tired of being mistreated by me, and didn't appreciate my off-the-cuff analysis; she wasn't going to take it anymore. She demanded to know what was up with me. As I was about to interpret her negative reaction as transference, one member said that I was analyzing her in the service of my aggression. The group, too, demanded to know what was up. I was immediately reminded of the writing of Karen Maroda (1999), who talked about therapist transparency. She said that there was a distinction between a therapist's judicious and timely use of feelings and the revelation of facts of their lives. I decided in that instant to tell the truth about my feelings. I told her I was confusing her with my old girlfriend. Unwittingly, I saw them as one and had taken out my frustrations on her. Her reaction, and the group's, was a reality check for me. There was a collective sigh of relief and an immediate release of tension in the room. I could actually see her face soften. I had validated her feeling that it was me that was inappropriate here and not her. She, with the group's support, had disrupted a potential "gaslighting" scenario. I could have tried to undermine her perception through the inherent power that the role of therapist provides. But the group would not let it happen. My subjective countertransference stood out so clearly that even I could see it.

4. THE PASS-ALONG EFFECT, OR DUMPING

You Learn What You Do

This happens when the leader passes on his or her pathology to group members. Both Gabbard (1995) and Langs (1982) have noted a similar phenomenon in individual psychotherapy. David Sedgwick (1994) describes Jung's concept of countertransference, which includes the unconscious reading of the therapist by the patient. Group members may "read" the leader's unconscious and act out such unspoken feelings as greed and entitlement in their own lives. This phenomenon is a form of projective identification in which patients incorporate the leader's pathology into their own behavior.

The noted educator, John Dewey, once said that you learn what you do. While he wasn't necessarily referring to the training of contemporary group therapists, he might well have been, because in order to become an effective group leader the neophyte group therapist must have the experience of being a group patient himself or herself. Coupled with group supervision of his work, the beginning group leader absorbs in vivo the theory, technique, style, assumptions, philosophy, and ethics of the senior leaders with whom he chooses to affiliate. He then imparts this intellectual, and also emotional, way of being in the world onto the population of group patients at large. It seems unimaginable to me that someone could become a competent group leader solely by reading a book or taking an academic course or two.

For example, a colleague who only practiced individual therapy, and who had never been a group patient himself, informed me that he intended to start a group. When I questioned the wisdom of attempting to run a group without having had any training in group, he assured me that he would do fine. He said that he was reading a book on how to run a therapy group. To his chagrin, the group never got off the ground. While he was able to convince some patients from his private practice to join, the group folded in less than a month (Pepper, 2014a).

One might think that professional group therapists would know better, but they don't necessarily. Just as self-indulgence and emotional hunger often motivate the senior leader's decisions, so do these feelings motivate their subordinates' behavior. This is a particularly pernicious scenario when the group members, who are group therapists themselves, pass along their pathology to the general population of group patients (Pepper, 2013).

In some analytic group training institutes, for example, "favored children" can receive valuable gifts from the revered senior leader. The gifts are symbolic rewards for loyalty to the system, and for a willingness to surrender critical thinking about the senior leader's behavior in exchange for the gratification of living a charmed life. Loyal disciples are often given patient referrals, teaching and administrative positions at the institute, opportunities to represent the organization at professional conferences, and chances to publish in the institute journal. A culture of greed pervades the atmosphere.

In such groups, however, the great power imbalances of families of origin are re-created and reenacted but not analyzed. As noted above, these dual relationships tend to be emotionally incestuous. And as with other types of incest constitute an abuse of power, they both exploit the vulnerability of the dependent person (Pepper, 2002). In the following scenario, a colleague of mine, who was in group therapy with a leader who raised the fee twice within a short period of time, largely for subjective reasons, did the same thing herself to the therapy group that she ran. Her behavior disrupted the group process.

In earlier articles (Pepper, 2003a, 2004b), I wrote about the intricacies of raising group fees. My colleague "Mary," the leader of a psychoanalytic therapy group, had been in group treatment with a leader who had raised the fee twice within a six-month period. Angry at her leader's seemingly greedy decision, Mary announced to her *own* group that the fee would be raised the following week.

After a short discussion about the impending increase, the matter was dropped. That night, immediately after the group, the members broke the leader's rule about outside group contact. They met at a local diner and, over dinner, the group discussed the impending fee increase among themselves.

In much the same way as her own group therapist had done, this leader had acted on subjective motives for raising the fee. Perhaps Mary was using the group to act out feelings of revenge against her own group leader. In any case, in not adequately preparing the group for an increase, she had actually precipitated a group resistance. The group may have perceived the sudden change in the contract as a frame violation. The members responded in kind. Meeting outside of the group was clearly an act of passive group defiance. The unspoken message could be read as: "Who needs you? If you exploit us, we'll meet without you!" Mary had violated her own rule about putting feelings into words and not into action. The group complied with her during the group session but chose to act out their feelings of aggression toward Mary through their rebellious behavior. On the other hand, not all fee increases are disruptive to the group process. In groups where the leader adequately readies members for an increase, acting out does not occur (Pepper, 2004b).

In another case of dumping, an experienced and psychologically sophisticated therapist in a complicated and competitive dual relationship with her own group therapist, used her connection to a travel agent (who was also her patient) to book herself upscale vacations.

As an added instance, in a supervision group of group therapists in which I was a member, the leader had convoluted dual relationships with many of the members. One such member presented a case where his own supervisee asked for a fee reduction. The presenter complied with the request, only to learn subsequently that his supervisee had been charging more than that reduced fee for his own services to his own patients, one of whom was the supervisee's own dentist! What happened next was both amusing and appalling.

The supervision group leader didn't bat an eye when he heard about this bizarre arrangement. Instead, he focused on the matter of the fee. No one attended to the wisdom and ethics of treating one's own dentist. Who was the patient here?

I wondered if the presenter's supervisee trusted his patient's unconscious enough to allow him into his mouth. What if the patient/dentist "accidentally" dropped an instrument down his throat, or gave him too much or too little Novocain? Then what?

I took issue with the direction that the discussion was going and raised a question about the negative effects on the transference and countertransference of this contaminated treatment relationship. My questions angered the leader, particularly when I referred to the treatment relationship as contaminated; the implication was that I was critical of both him and the presenter for failing to address the issue of boundaries. In a loud and commanding tone, the leader turned to the presenter and said, "Beware of obsessive-compulsive therapists who insist on aseptic boundaries in treatment." I had been effectively silenced; and the group passively returned to offering the presenter concrete suggestions about the fee.

The fact that group supervision leader himself had engaged in complicated dual relationships with patients that blinded him to the reality of my colleague's crazy treatment arrangement. The leader couldn't help him because they shared a delusion, a *folie a deux*. The presenter was providing substandard care to his supervisees and our group leader was tacitly condoning it. In fact, there was a parallel process between our leader's behavior and that of my groupmates. Both were supporting an egregious boundary violation, which was being passed on to the general population of group therapy patients.

5. OVERSTIMULATION

This happens when the leader's transparency becomes too gratifying for all participants. The group therapist puts his or her own needs ahead of the group's needs, which leads to problematic consequences to the therapy. Unwilling or unable to think through the implications of his conduct, the leader morphs therapy into not-therapy. As a result, group members are overwhelmed, flooded with emotions toward the leader that are largely unwanted and largely ignored. Complicated emotions are not addressed because the unspoken message of overstimulation in group is that indulgence is valued over the analysis. The gratification spurs the creation of a conspiracy of silence. Group members adopt the leader's tacit value system but are not emotionally equipped to metabolize all the feelings induced in them by the leader. This can have a catastrophic impact on the treatment. I have always been fascinated by this process and have wondered how leaders justify their own actions. The unanswered question here is: How is their behavior therapeutic for the group and its members? More often than not, it isn't.

I have observed (Pepper, 2003a) that this phenomenon frequently occurs when group leaders run their groups from their home. This is particularly the case where the treatment room is not physically separated from the living quarters. While the potential for overstimulation is more intense in a group setting, it can be quite provocative in an individual treatment setting as well.

In the following example from my own personal experience in individual therapy, the treatment environment was so confusing as a result of the clinician's own narcissistic need that a collusion of silence between patient and therapist occurred. There was too much gratification in not attending to the reality of the seductive scene and, even though no physical contact took place, neither participant was willing to give it up, and as a result the therapy suffered for it. The therapist avoided having to examine her need to act out her exhibitionism and the patient avoided having to consciously experience his anger at being sexually stirred in treatment.

When I was a neophyte therapist, I was in treatment with an attractive woman whose office was in her posh Fifth Avenue apartment. The treatment room was separated from her living quarters by beautiful stained glass doors. I sat facing her with the doors behind her. Often she would leave the doors ajar so that I could peer into her boudoir on the other side. Her intimate female apparel was clearly visible, draped over the back of the chair at her dressing table. Although it was very provocative, I never said anything about it! And she didn't ask. I didn't say anything because I was afraid that she'd close the doors. This taught me a valuable lesson: The patient's needs should always come first.

In this case, her behavior was overstimulating and a distraction. Beneath the titillation, I was angry and lost respect for her turning therapy into not-therapy. She had interfered with my saying everything. I realized that this was end of treatment but stayed anyway for some months and we wound up playing an unspoken game of: "Let's not attend to what's really going on here." A quote from R. D. Laing (1970) seems apt here:

> They are playing a game. They are playing at not playing a game. If I show them I see they are, I shall break the rules and they will punish me. I must play their game, of not seeing I see the game. (Laing, 1970, p. 1)

One might ask why this scenario occurred in the first place. I believe that, in addition to character flaws of individual players, the potentiality for enactment increases in a blurred-boundary environment. It is the combination of these two factors that can produce volatility in the treatment.

I am certain that, if she had been asked, my therapist would have agreed that the patient's needs always come first. However, once a boundary was crossed, as in this case where the living quarters were adjacent to her boudoir, the door was open (pun intended) to the interference of unanalyzed and unrestrained impulses that are largely destructive to the treatment.

In another case, a colleague of mine, who ran his group practice from his suburban home, called me one day to complain about what a group member of his *almost* did to my colleague's family dog. My colleague presented himself as a victim but in reality had been fully complicit in setting up the conditions for the playing out of this near-tragedy. He didn't see his part in it. Here's what happened.

My colleague, the group leader, felt badly for the member, a professional who had become unemployed. In an apparent act of kindness, the leader agreed to employ the group member as a dog walker for the family pooch. The first day on the job, however, the leader watched in horror as the member was about to offer the dog a piece of chocolate. As many dog lovers know, chocolate can be poisonous to a dog. My colleague carped about what almost happened to his pet. While listening to the story, though, I saw it differently and debated with myself as to whether I should tell my colleague what I thought—that it wasn't entirely the group member's fault.

It occurred to me that perhaps the member/dog walker was ignorant and didn't know the potential danger. But I also thought that my colleague's apparent act of kindness may have unconsciously been perceived by the member as a form of bragging, as Maroda (1999) has noted in her article about therapists who run their practices in their upscale homes. It was as if the leader were saying, "Look how much I have and you don't. You are so beneath me that the best you can do is to walk my dog" The very act of the therapist paying for the dog-walking service in itself confounds the treatment relationship.

According to Langs (1982), the giving of gifts by the therapist to the patient (the hiring of the patient in this case, for example) is unconsciously seen by the patient as dangerous.

> It blurs the boundaries between patient and therapist, and ultimately deprives the patient of what is needed from the therapist. At the very moment that a therapist gives a patient a gift, the deep unconscious system experiences a dramatic sense of deprivation, loss and harm (Langs, 1989, p. 187).

Perhaps, in a twisted act of revenge, the member unconsciously acted out her murderous rage toward the therapist by attempting to kill the leader's dog. I would imagine that the patient must have felt quite guilty about the thought that she could have injured the dog. Was it in the best interest of the patient's treatment to have had these feelings, or to have been put in this predicament in the first place? I think not.

One might wonder why an intelligent and experienced clinician would be willing to jeopardize so much by undertaking an obviously destructive and self-destructive action. As in the first example, behavior is always multidimensional and, once again, there are probably several factors that might explain his behavior. First, a flaw in the leader's character, an inability to anticipate the ramifications of his actions, fueled by a narcissistic and competitive need to outshine his patient, might account for the blind spot. But it might also be that the group leader's own training, which was characterized by lack of appropriate boundaries, explains the rest of it. He was schooled at an institute at which group members and the leader had a myriad of complicated dual relationships with each other, and where gratification was valued above analysis. This, combined with the leader's own personality quirk, could lead to a gross insensitivity to frame issues. Under such circumstances, boundary violations can readily occur.

The irony is that the possibility of resolving the character flaw in the arena of group therapy is forestalled by the very social structure of the treatment environment where the existence of complicated multiple relationships is syntonic with the pathological narcissism of the members and leaders alike.

This episode reminds me of the ethical debacle that ensued after Stanley Milgram's (1963) notorious experiment *Obedience,* where he placed unsuspecting subjects in the position of believing they had done serious harm to other people, when in fact they hadn't. Actually the harm that was done was to them. They were forced to wonder what kind of people they really were to have blindly followed the experimenter's orders to hurt others. After this incident, research organizations developed strict guidelines as to what constituted ethical experiment protocols.

In another case of overstimulation, a group member, a lay person with experience as an accountant, was asked by his own analytic institute-affiliated group therapist to serve as a bookkeeper for the organization. The member felt flattered by the offer and immediately accepted it without consideration of its potential downside. But was it the member's responsibility to foresee danger here? No, obviously not. It was the group leader's place to protect the integrity of the treatment; but gratification got in the way of his professional responsibility.

In fact, the group member-turned-institute-accountant derived a great sense of satisfaction from having been invited to serve in this capacity. He felt special in his treatment group, having a privileged status that the other members didn't have. There was also secondary-gain gratification for this patient; a feeling of power over the professionals, whom he saw as incompetent to perform this task for themselves. The patient felt contempt for his group therapist as a result, but this was not discussed in the treatment group. He experienced too much pleasure from this guilty secret to make it public. He saw no reason to talk about it, and in this way was overstimulated. Needless to say, not talking about all this had a deleterious effect on the treatment because not talking about feelings often can be emotionally destabilizing.

This example illustrates two ways in which the transference was undermined through dual relationships. First, the member experienced too much gratification from the role reversal. Instead of being in a subordinate relationship to the group leader, the group patient felt superior, as the expert. *Who was dependent on whom?*

To have talked about it, the group member would have had to be willing to let it go. Since the leader did not address the convoluted change in the treatment relationship and its potential damage to the therapy, the group member took the group therapist's lead and followed the unspoken message—gratification was valued over analysis. He contained all this and in that way acquiesced to the status quo. However, the group member felt overwhelmed, having to contain all these hidden feelings, and subsequently became depressed and anxious because he had to contain more than just feelings of gratification. There was a darker side to all this.

The failure of the leader to take responsibility for potentially harming the treatment through the creation of this dual relationship led the member to feel unconscious contempt, for which the patient felt simultaneously guilty and gleeful. Second, the patient was reluctant to share his nether side with the group, lest he be perceived as ungrateful for having been granted this special status to the leader. He feared the group's judgment and loss of the leader's approbation. As a consequence, all of this was submerged but it was too much for the member to bear. He subsequently put these feelings into his body and developed symptoms. He rightly felt exploited but felt helpless to extricate himself from this mess.

I never found out if the patient was actually paid for his work as an accountant. The issue of financial compensation could only have complicated an already chaotic arrangement. How was the rate of compensation determined, anyway? Did the leader lower the member's group fee in lieu of compensation? Or was he paid directly by the leader? Either way would have had meaning for the member that would have exacerbated the symptoms since he had no business serving as his therapist's bookkeeper in the first place. Then I had a funny but dark thought; *What if he had skimmed money off the top?* Overstimulation can also occur when a group member is too close to the leader and, although the closeness isn't physical, the effects can still be damaging for the patient.

For example, at an open-house meeting of a Modern Analytic training institute, run by a charismatic leader, an attractive young woman "hawked" the program to a large audience (Pepper, 1992). Giving testimony to the personal power and wisdom of the leader, "Natalie" told the assembly that, as a consequence of her treatment with him, she had grown in ways she had never thought possible. Listening to this, I thought that she sounded like a disciple of a guru proselytizing for a cult. The idealized transference was presented as a statement of fact. The implicit message was that, through association with the revered leader, prospective students would be able to identify with his strength of character. That the idealization could be a form of projective identification never was addressed. It had been accepted without question.

In fact, I knew Natalie personally and knew that she was one of the leader's favorites. And while she held a special status in that group, she also paid a high price for it; the transference had become an overstimulating reality. In her real life, she had been the favorite of a powerful and seductive father. Here it was being played out in her therapy. One consequence of this was that "her heart belonged to Daddy." She never married. Natalie had great difficulty making healthy choices in her romantic life, often choosing married men as lovers, men whom she could never have for herself. It seemed to me to be a tragic case of the leader's narcissism being gratified at her expense. He couldn't or wouldn't let her go, as her father didn't, and she was doomed to a lonely life.

The Temerlins (1982) noted a similar phenomenon in their study of psychotherapy cults in the Midwest. While this type of incestuous connection to the leader provides the member with a false sense of personal power and well-being, ultimately it undermines the treatment and also interferes with the development of strong attachments to significant others in real life. Emotional loyalty is reserved for the leader and the psychological family (Temerlin & Temerlin, 1982).

6. THE EMPEROR'S NEW CLOTHES EFFECT

This occurs when the group colludes with the leader to protect him from too close scrutiny of his character flaws. Gabbard (1995) notes that: "the idealization of senior colleagues may create situations reminiscent of the fairy tale *The Emperor's New Clothes*, in which otherwise intelligent analysts disbelieve or rationalize what they see in plain view" (p. 95). Sometimes this phenomenon can reach literal and even comical proportions; a real-life story about Dr. Hyman Spotnitz, the founder of the Modern school, is an example.

There were conflicting stories about him. He was brilliant but he could also be intimidating, sadistic, and aggressive. I had admired his writings and was intrigued but torn about studying with him. Before passing judgment, I wanted to find out about this man for myself. So when I heard that he would be leading a public discussion and demonstration group of his techniques, I signed up. The lecture took place in a large auditorium with a stage where a circle of chairs had been set up. When he came out on stage, one thing stood out over all else. He was wearing a funny red wig. Here he was on a stage with eight members of a demonstration group, running the group wearing a bright red wig that made him look like a buffoon. Here was a great example of the "emperor's new clothes" effect, I thought. He looked like a schmuck. *So, let's see what happens,* I wondered. Would anyone in the group confront him on his appearance? The answer was no. *No one said anything about the way he looked.* I said to myself, "How could anyone be afraid of this guy? He didn't look at all intimidating, quite the opposite. It would be easy to say negative things about him. He looked like a foolish and vain old man." Still, I was curious and decided to call to set up an in-person meeting. But when I finally summoned up the courage to call him, I was told that he was about to retire and was not taking on any new trainees.

Years later, a longtime associate of his told me that Dr. Spotnitz felt self-conscious about being bald but he didn't want to wear a hat lest people thought him to be an orthodox Jew. I thought, *So what if they did?* Was this guy so insecure that he cared what others thought of him for wearing a hat? But who knows? I got this tidbit secondhand.

The "emperor's new clothes" effect isn't always so garish. Sometimes this phenomenon is more subtle in the way that it plays out, occurring in groups where members simply overlook the behavior of leaders who ignore reality. In the following vignette, a colleague told me of a group that she joined in which members overlooked the behavior of their co-leaders.

In a training group at an analytic institute, these leaders gave special treatment to a female member who was a close relation of the clinic director. The woman, middle-aged and single, habitually complained about her life. She was unhappy, wanted to marry and have children; she complained bitterly about her personal relations. She even complained about the group room. It wasn't good enough for her. The lighting was poor, the ventilation was inadequate, and on and on. Group members suffered her in silence and the leaders allowed her great latitude in her complaints, never asking her if she were unhappy with them and the all-female group as well. My colleague said that she studied the group dynamics, reluctant as a newcomer to question what she saw.

Things changed one day when a male member joined the group. A man in his mid-fifties, handsome, and polite, he attracted her attention. She was clearly interested in him but the feeling wasn't mutual. He found her insufferable, as did the women. He flatly told her, "You suck the air out of the room." With that, the group fell eerily silent. No one said anything, even the leaders, who in their silence tacitly threw him under the bus by shirking their responsibility to address the gorilla in the room. The new male member was furious with them for coddling the chronic complainer, and he said so. She was untouchable because they allowed it to happen.

The group, *and the leaders*, walked on eggshells because she was related to their boss, the clinic director. They were all afraid. Ultimately the buck stopped with the leaders. It was incumbent upon them to confront the unspoken conspiracy in the room. The members took their cue from the leaders. Their inaction said it all. There was lifelessness to the group that was never addressed. The male member dropped out of the group not long after joining. The leaders' passivity contributed to a group collusion to avoid confronting this woman on her off-putting behavior. The inertia of the group overrode the male member. There are also cases of the "Emperor's New Clothes" effect that are egregious.

In Chapter 4, I noted that Gabbard & Lester (1995) observed the "Emperor's New Clothes" effect at individual psychoanalytic training institutes run by grandiose administrators. In a previous section, I mentioned my own experience with an unsavory clinic director whom I worked for in my early days as a therapist.

I was in a treatment group run by a leader who was simultaneously an administrator at the clinic (Dr. K), and many of the group members were fellow staff therapists with me at that clinic. Once again, I originally published a vignette about this event from the perspective of an outside observer. In fact, it was an event that I personally witnessed (Pepper, 1990).

One evening a new member joined the group. She was someone that I knew from the clinic, another staff therapist. That night, she told the group a harrowing tale. She was on the verge of a nervous breakdown because of her crazy relationship with the clinic director (I called him Dr. J.), who, as it turned out, was not only her boss but also her individual therapist. She said that he referred patients to her private practice on the condition that she split the patients' fees with him and, in addition, had sex with him. Now she wanted out of this incestuous arrangement but didn't have the strength to do so. She said that she was in group with the hope that the group would help her find a way out.

The group was appalled by what we heard. Some of us in the group who worked at the clinic knew that Dr. J. and Dr. K. were personal friends as well as colleagues. Although we had no way of knowing whether her allegations could be substantiated, as clinicians we knew that Dr. K. had an ethical responsibility to report the matter to the professional organization that he and Dr. J. were both members of. To my knowledge, he never did.

I had to question Dr. K.'s personal integrity. If he could remain in association with Dr. J. after what the group was hearing, I reasoned, and not report him, then what kind of person was *he*? For Dr. K. to do nothing, was to tacitly condone Dr. J.'s egregious behavior. But the group rallied around him. The consensus was that the clinic director's character bore no reflection on our group leader. Most group members saw no reason to believe that Dr. K.'s unwillingness to alert the ethics committee was an act of complicity. I strongly disagreed and, shortly thereafter, I quit that group, quit the clinic, and severed all contact with both men.

This seems to be a clear example of a case of the "emperor's new clothes." The group was willing to overlook the egregious behavior of both Dr. J and Dr. K. I would suspect that this group collusion took place in an effort not to jeopardize members' own interests, risking the loss of the leader's approbation. The status quo was preserved, even when it was at the expense of a fellow group member's mental health.

7. SCAPEGOATING

The term *scapegoat* comes from the Hebrew "goat of Azazel." During the ritual of the Day of Atonement in ancient times, a goat was sacrificed as a symbolic purging of the sins of the Jews (Scheidlinger, 1982). As it applies to group therapy today, the term is used to describe a process in which a member is singled out as the target of the group's scorn. According to contemporary research, there seem to be at least two causes of scapegoating; 1) Scheidlinger and others (Moreno, 2007; Gabbard, 2005) have argued that scapegoating is a form of projective identification in which the scapegoater externalizes unwanted self-parts. Moreno says, "In this way, the projected material is less toxic and easier to manage insofar as it is 'not me'" (p. 95); 2) Ormont believed that scapegoating is a displacement of aggression away from the group therapist (Ormont, 1974). This happens when the group turns anger intended for the leader onto a weak member (Pepper, 1990, 2003).

For example, I once became a member of a training group where one female member was not charged a fee. The group was not aware of this fact before I joined but we learned of it shortly thereafter. It came to the group's attention that the leader had allowed her special treatment because she claimed to be broke. The two of them had kept this arrangement a secret. When the details came to light, the group's anger and jealousy were directed at her. She was the scapegoat until I spoke up and said that the leader was to blame here, for two reasons: 1) the arrangement was a secret, making it appear incestuous; 2) even if he had charged her one dollar for the therapy, it would have at least been a symbolic acknowledgment of their professional relationship. Actually, charging her nothing was demeaning the value of the treatment for her. The leader was unconsciously saying that his services weren't worth very much. Further, how could she possibly say anything when she was so grateful to him, so special in his eyes? And he lost the group's respect for having put her in this position. For my part, I promptly quit that group. The point here is that the leader is ultimately responsible for everything that occurs in group.

Whether the scapegoating occurs because of projective identification or displacement, in either case it is the leader's responsibility to direct the aggression back on himself or herself. The emotional well-being of the scapegoated depends upon it. After all, the leader is the common link between all group members and is responsible for the composition of the group. If the group, or any of its members, has a problem with another member, it was the leader who brought them together. But in a blurred boundary environment, it may be too difficult to know what is exactly going on.

For example, in an article about gossiping by Gans (2014), he provides a vignette of gossip as the scapegoating of an absent group member. The incident occurred in a T-group of psychiatric residents. The others resented one of the members, "Harold," because he wasn't carrying his fair share of clinical responsibilities. Further, he was selected by the residency training director for a special assignment. The group gossiped about him when he was not in attendance at meetings. Wisely, the leader focused on the here and now of the group experience—who was doing their fair share of the work in the T-group? According to Gans, this resolved the problem. What the author doesn't address, however, perhaps because he didn't see it, was the role played in this scenario by Harold's special status in the larger organization and the real-life sibling rivalry that most likely existed between him and the other residents. The scapegoating of Harold may have been as much about the others' jealousy as about gossip. Given their dual relationships as students in the residency program and T-group members, the resentment of the others may have been a displacement of their anger at the director of the residency program, and the group leader as a representative of the program, for showing preferential treatment to one of their group members. The chance of scapegoating occurring, where dual relationships exist in training programs, may be higher than many participants realize.

For another example in Rosenthal (1992), the author describes a situation in a training group seminar where older members attempted to rid the group of a newcomer by complaining about the effectiveness of the group and its leader. He writes: "The aim of this group defamation campaign is to convince the intruder that this is not the right group and that he or she would do well to look elsewhere for group treatment" (Rosenthal, 1992, p. 280). But in fact this was not a treatment group. It was a group therapy seminar where the leader ran it *like* a treatment group; members were expected to share their feelings toward each other and the leader. In the end, the new member left the group anyway; but not necessarily as Rosenthal reasoned. He believed that the group's behavior was a form of infanticide, an attempt to kill off the "newborn." But there's another way to look at this.

In light of the blurred boundaries between treatment and training, the group may have actually been protecting the new member and scapegoating her at the same time. Since this was a training group, and assumedly members had outside contact, it would have been unwise for members to speak too freely about their feelings toward each other. Who knows what real life consequences of looping could have occurred? It might have been that members were actually angry at the leader for having turned a didactic seminar into a treatment group. So when, Rosenthal reports, "she doggedly resisted his invitation to share her feelings with the group" (p. 280), it may have been that, rather than resisting, she may have had the good sense to leave a group that made her feel "just too uncomfortable" (Rosenthal, 1992, p. 280).

The interpretation of this group process as infanticide may have been a rationalization. Here scapegoating was masquerading as another case of the "emperor's new clothes" effect, in which the leader and the members conspire to direct the anger away from him for having compromised the integrity of the training seminar's boundaries. It seems to me that the leader/therapist was being protected by the group at the expense of the newcomer.

As an aside, a former supervisor of mine once said, half-jokingly, that the definition of resistance is anything that the patient does that the therapist doesn't like. Scapegoating can also occur in other types of altered frame environments as well.

For instance, at a recent meeting of professional group therapists, one leader presented a case of scapegoating in group (Pepper, 2013). The presenter described a group dynamic in which the men in her group were abusive and overly aggressive with an attractive female member, whom the men characterized as arrogant and unapproachable. The presenter's focus was to elucidate what her role was in exacerbating the situation. According to the presenter, she acted out an induced countertransference in which she played the female member's neglectful mother. However, at the end of the presentation, and almost as an aside, the presenter mentioned that the group met in the living room of her home, with photos of her family around the room. It occurred to at least one observer that the fact that the group met in the leader's home may have contributed to the scapegoating process. It may have been that the men in the group were actually quite angry with the leader for her overstimulating them with too much information about her personal life, and perhaps even felt jealous of the leader's flaunting her primary attachment to her real-life family that the photos around the room symbolized. Hence they displaced their unconscious aggression toward the leader onto a vulnerable female in the group.

REVIEW

Boundary crossings are not inherently boundary violations. However, we have seen time and again, altering the frame of analytic group therapy always has an impact on the treatment. Boundary violations constitute an abuse of power. In this way, boundary violations betray the members' trust that the practitioner is an ethical leader. They occur when the leader alters the frame of analytic treatment to such an extent that members experience iatrogenic treatment reactions. These reactions can occur in a variety of ways, hence the seven dangers.

1. BREACHES OF CONFIDENTIALITY: when the leader fosters dual relationships in group that by definition constitute breaches of group member privacy, as in Suzy's case, where her decision to leave treatment became public knowledge.

2. LOOPING: when information presented in one context rebounds back onto the presenter in another, as was my predicament when I interviewed with a fellow group member who doubled as my boss.
3. THE PASS ALONG EFFECT: when senior leaders pass on their own pathology to their students and then the general population of group members, as in the case of Mary, who arbitrarily raised her group's fee after her own group therapist greedily raised her group fee twice within a six-month period;
4. OVERSTIMULATION: when the leader's transparency goes too far, overgratifying members' incestuous fantasies about the group therapist's personal life, as was the case of the female therapist who left the doors ajar;
5. GASLIGHTING: when the leader blames members for treatment impasses, as in the case of Melvin, who was told that his negative feelings toward the leader were transference after they wrote a book together.
6. 'THE EMPEROR'S NEW CLOTHES EFFECT': when the group protects the leader from close scrutiny, as was the case of Dr. Spotnitz's group that didn't comment on his wearing a silly red wig.
7. SCAPEGOATING: when the group displaces its aggression onto a weak member, as was the case of the T-group member who was the subject of gossip because he was treated specially by the director of the residency program.

The underlying hazard of all these dangers is that the leader's behavior interferes with the members' willingness and ability to adhere to the treatment contract, which in group therapy is: "Put all of your thoughts and feelings toward other members, and why you feel that way, into words." This creates an atmosphere in which it isn't safe to say everything, and a conspiracy of silence ensues, often with the development of symptoms in vulnerable members.

When negative treatment reactions are manifested during the course of analytic group psychotherapy, it is rare that the frame of the treatment is considered first as the source of the problem. Whether the negative treatment reaction is understood as members' transference or an entire group resistance or anything in between, a psychoanalytic explanation is most likely to be used to understand the phenomenon. The implicit assumption is that most of the responsibility for the impasse lies with the member, or the group, and that the impasses take the form of resistance and transference.

In fact, among analysts, there is an informal rule of thumb about transference that is referred to as the 10 Percent Rule. This rule has been applied to group treatment as well. It is based upon the belief that group members' perceptions of the leader are most likely a distortion, and area result of historical artifacts that skew their view of the present reality. However, it is also assumed that the group's or individual member's negative perceptions are not always distorted and that, roughly speaking, their observations of the group therapist are objectively accurate about 10 percent of the time.

The implicit understanding among group therapists, in other words, is that the bias is away from the leader. Subjective countertransference is not generally considered first to be a significant variable in the equation. Consequently, iatrogenesis is not thought of as the source of negative treatment reactions. However, it is my thesis that, under certain conditions, this supposition may constitute a serious error in judgment. Operating under the 10 Percent Rule in instances where boundaries are blurred may have significant negative consequences for individual members and the group in general.

Leaders who alter the frame of treatment bear an added burden to their professional obligation to their groups. It is incumbent upon any group leader who chooses to blur boundaries to take greater responsibility for treatment impasses. These leaders must be eternally vigilant to consider the frame of treatment first in any such impasses. To do otherwise is to place their group member in emotional and even, at times, physical jeopardy.

Chapter Six

Other People's Stories

This chapter is devoted to a presentation of the untoward blurred-boundary group experiences that some brave individuals have chosen to share with me. In response to professional listserv requests and personal invitations, group members, both professional group therapists and laypeople in their own group treatment have revealed their stories about the muddling of the line between group therapy and not-therapy. The events presented below have taken place in groups of a variety of theoretical orientations such psychoanalytic, modern analytic, ego analytic, object relations, self-psychology, and gestalt.

While the groups differ in their leaders' approach to treatment, they are similar in at least one important respect—in each group there existed a culture that tacitly supported and maintained a conspiracy of silence. Although no one explicitly forbade the discussion of the effects of the blurred boundaries in these groups, members implicitly complied with the unspoken directive. The potential damage of a compromised treatment environment is compounded when it remains unaddressed.

I contacted one group leader who posted a listserv advertisement announcing that he was starting a therapy group exclusively for group therapists. My goal was to interview him for this book, in order to learn what he thought the pros and cons of running such a group would be, both for him and for group members. Since it was highly likely that members would have contact with him and with each other outside the group, it seemed like a perfect opportunity to understand the complications of establishing these dual relationships as the process was about to unfold.

Initially, the leader was open to the idea of being interviewed but couldn't seem to commit to a time and place to meet. It occurred to me that he was of two minds about being interviewed. I wondered about his resistance to talking. In frustration, I asked if he had changed his mind about the interview. He said that he'd like to take a pass on it at this time. Could it be that the topic was too threatening for him to address in public? But he was not the only one who was reluctant to speak.

Not all of the stories of the group members that I interviewed are presented here. Despite my assurances that identifying information would be disguised, some interviewees decided not to go public. Of course, I have respected their requests; but I was not surprised by their change of heart.

Some had second thoughts about coming forward, lest the group and its leader recognize themselves. There was a fear of reprisal but only a vague sense of what specific danger existed. These members were quite paranoid that there would be retribution for their disloyalty to their group's expectation of silence.

In a follow-up interview, for example, one interviewee recanted what he had told me, downplaying the significance of the offense and asked me not to publish it. This man was clearly quite conflicted about his attachment to the leader. Although he felt wronged, he also loved his group therapist and felt protective of him.

Most of those who changed their minds, however, were not so much concerned about the reactions of their offending group leader; they were concerned that their fellow group members might recognize themselves and take umbrage with the interviewee's audacity. These claimants identified with the potential hurt and embarrassment that their disclosure of their group dynamics might cause, and worried that they might be ostracized for it. Despite the fact that they were the injured parties, they felt guilty about the exposure of their emotional truth.

This only adds further validity to the concept of regression in group (Freud, 1921) and the concomitant power of the conspiracy of silence. Like the incest survivor who feels guilty about betraying the family secret, some of the interviewees felt a childlike sense of unfaithfulness when they talked to me. In their regressed state, they saw themselves as the betrayers of the leader and the group. Their sense of culpability overwhelmed them, perhaps in the same way that they felt guilty in their family of origin for feeling anger toward an offending parent or sibling.

It is my conjecture that their strong feelings of paranoia, which were based on fear, derived from guilt about feeling angry. We know that children can be exceedingly loyal to a dysfunctional family system, even to the point of turning the aggression back onto themselves.

In fact, some of the interviewees confided that they had become depressed as a result of their experience but didn't understand why, that is, not until they talked about it. They blamed themselves for the treatment impasse. Though adult and competent, in the regressed state of a group member these interviewees were remorseful about the public exposure of their emotional injury.

As a metaphor, when a physical wound is not healing properly, sometimes the recommended treatment is to open the wound and clean it out so that it may heal correctly. It might be said that the open airing of the conspiracy of silence that plagues these groups needs to be addressed for the healing process to begin. This chapter is a step in that direction, toward that goal, a brief discussion of group dynamics in general.

THE POWER OF GROUP TO DEFINE REALITY

The anthropologist Weston La Barre was known to have said: "The only difference between a culture and schizophrenia is that in a culture more than one person believes it" (in Slater, 1974, p. 50). In other words, reality is a variable; it is a social construct. To my mind, the old adage '"Seeing is believing" is actually the other way round: "Believing is seeing." If an individual doesn't believe something is real, he won't see it. The same principle applies to groups. A group culture by definition is shared; it is therefore the group's reality. This truism applies to the "culture" of therapy groups as well.

A major theme of this book has been the group's ability to create, maintain, and enforce its own truth. While groups may differ in their value systems, they essentially employ similar interpersonal dynamics to control members. That is, members abide by the rules to obtain the leader and the group's approbation, or suffer the consequences, be they withdrawal of affection or worse (Neurath, 2005). Two famous studies immediately come to mind from among many others. Solomon Asch's (1951) paper on the effects of group pressure on perception and Leon Festinger's (1956) *When Prophecy Fails*.

In the Asch experiment, groups of strangers were able to alter the perception of reality of unsuspecting subjects through group influence. In the Festinger study, members of a cult that was led by a floridly psychotic woman were able to maintain a delusional belief system even in the face of stark reality. The power of a group to shield the leader from close scrutiny, the "emperor's new clothes" effect, is often at the heart of a conspiracy of silence.

Both the good news and the bad news about group psychotherapy is that members must regress in order for the process to work (Freud, 1921). It is for this reason that I wrote, in a previous paper (Pepper, 1997), that the role of patient in an analytically oriented psychotherapy group is probably the most unequal of any adult relationship. Therapy group members are vulnerable to exploitation because the extreme power differential between member, group, and leader. On the other hand, effective treatment can only take place if the group willingly allows the leader to control the direction of interpersonal interactions.

In my therapy groups, for example, the contract is that members are expected to say how they feel toward the other members and why they feel that way. When my groups are functioning at an optimal level, members hold each other accountable to that contract when they veer off into advice-giving or worse, name-calling, and character assassination. Members remind each other to state their feelings before offering their thoughts. The members' inclination to adopt to this value system, at least during the time that they are in group, is a testament to the human tendency to become attached to a group and its leader and follow the spoken and/or unspoken principles laid down by the therapist. This point was made very clear in a recent discussion with a former patient/student of a famous group leader.

Francine's Story

A group therapist, a middle-aged woman in group treatment with a charismatic and grandiose leader, told me that the leader placed her in the same group as her older sister. My informant had passively acquiesced but confessed that she didn't like that arrangement. It reiterated the dynamic of her original family, in which the older sibling was the favored child. In fact, the experience was so disruptive to their already strained relationship that a long period of total estrangement followed. When I asked her why she stayed in that group, she confided that she hadn't thought much about it until I asked the question. The group leader told her to do it, so she did. She said that it was as natural to follow his directive without question as it was to breathe the air. It was startling to hear that such an erudite woman could be so submissive and blindly compliant without thinking through the consequences. This seems to be a clear demonstration of the regressive power of group, particularly when led by a powerful leader.

Amy's Story

A group member, a layperson in treatment with a well-known leader, reported that a new member joined the group and immediately engendered the enmity of fellow members. The new member, a professional group therapist himself, made it clear from the start that he was different from the others in that he had a relationship with the leader outside the group. The group was consistently reminded of this fact each time he addressed her. For unlike all the other members who addressed the leader formally, the newcomer called her by her first name.

This group nuance, in and of itself, may have not had great significance except that the newcomer held himself apart in other ways as well. He came across in a supercilious manner, refusing to engage in positive and constructive dialogues with the rest of the group. The newcomer's informality with the leader was a symbolic reminder to the group of his superior and special status with her and the members resented him for it.

However, it is my belief that this resentment was in reality a displacement of anger away from the leader. Had the leader interpreted the group's reaction to the newcomer as transference, as sibling rivalry, then an egregious act would have occurred. Such an interpretation would have been gaslighting the group, because the reaction of the members was at least in part a response to the compromised treatment environment that was brought about by the leader's decision to bring someone that she knew socially into the group.

The newcomer was the scapegoat for the group's resentment toward the leader who had put her own needs first, ahead of the group's best interest. The group did not directly challenge the leader's decision. Members broke the rule of no outside contact and at a diner discussed the idea of them all quitting the group. The leader had actually precipitated this crisis. In breaking *her* own rule, the leader tacitly gave the group license to do the same. In the end, they chose to stay, but the compromise solution was to turn their antagonism onto the leader's colleague.

It is my impression that, in most instances, when an entire group has a negative reaction to a new member, this is an unspoken statement to the leader. It is an expression of the group's objection to the leader's decision to bring in the newcomer. Whether the objection is reality-based or not, the leader ultimately bears responsibility for all that happens in the group, including its composition.

Amy reported that the leader got the message that the group was not happy with the new member's behavior and had begun to point out when he behaved condescendingly. However, the underlying issue of the incestuous nature of his relationship to her had not been addressed. And as a consequence, an unreal atmosphere had settled upon the group, and progressive emotional communication came to a halt.

It would have been the leader's task to bravely ask the group if it had been her mistake to bring in this newcomer in the first place. That would have been the leader's ways of letting the group know that she was willing to talk openly about the now-compromised treatment milieu while providing the group with the opportunity to air their angry feelings toward her. Sadly, my informant has told me that he plans to quit the group rather than confront this issue with the leader in the group.

Ronnie's Story

Ronnie's therapist invited her to train at the institute where the clinician was on staff. As part of the training, students are required to participate in a treatment exercise in which they work intensely to resolve personal issues in front of an audience of senior clinicians; her therapist was part of that group. Ronnie felt guilty and disloyal to her own therapist when the clinician that she worked with was better able to help her than her own therapist, who watched their interaction. She felt like she was cheating on her therapist. Ronnie spared her therapist's feelings by not discussing any of this in therapy.

A Conspiracy of Silence: Sydney's Story

Sydney told me that she and a colleague shared the same therapist at the institute where they both trained. They have often discussed the therapist's style. Sydney believes that this has contaminated the work. For example, Sydney's colleague has confided to her that it's easy for him to hide out in his sessions with the shared therapist by not talking about his struggles at the institute. Sydney has judged their mutual therapist as inadequate because of this, questioning her ability to manage the dual relationships, none of which has been discussed in treatment by either Sydney or her colleague.

Meryl's Story

In another instance of dual relationships, Meryl, an institute trainee, reported that, as a faculty member, her own therapist has led training sessions, experiential interactions as well as demonstrations of individual sessions with students, in Meryl's presence. Her therapist can be a maternal figure; and Meryl reported that just like her biological mother, her therapist impinged on her autonomy. Meryl felt exposed and intruded upon having her therapist in her classes. She wanted to appear the perfect student and impress her. But this is all too stimulating for her, re-creating the original family scenario. Transference has become reality but none of this has been addressed in her treatment. Neither Meryl nor the therapist has addressed this complicated dynamic. Once again this is evidence of a conspiracy of silence.

Betrayal of a Confidence

Joannie told me that in an individual supervision setting, she revealed an error that she was ashamed of. The supervisor exposed the error at a supervision group meeting without getting Joannie's permission to discuss the case. She felt humiliated. She was anxious and cried when she told me the story. She had trusted that her supervisor would keep a confidence and so she felt betrayed.

Fear of Looping

Lauren participated in a demonstration session at her training institute in front of her fellow students, teachers, supervisors, and her own therapist. She was encouraged to reveal quite personal experiences and feelings but feared that, in doing so, she jeopardized her chances of future patient referrals. She worried that the others would judge her harshly, disclosing her most irrational emotions about her childhood memories in public. She regretted having revealed too much. She lamented that it wasn't a wise thing to do.

Carol's Story

A new patient of mine, Carol, told me that her last therapist practiced from her home office. It wasn't until we talked that she realized her discomfort with this arrangement was justified. For one thing, the clinician's mother lived in the house and would periodically appear in the foyer that doubled as a waiting room. The therapist's mother would sit down next to Carol and chat. She was very uncomfortable about these conversations but didn't want to appear rude to the woman. She never said anything about this to her therapist. She felt conflicted about talking because the therapist served her cappuccino while she waited (the therapist usually ran fifteen minutes late for sessions), and Carol didn't want to jeopardize what she experienced as her special status in the therapist's real-life family. It wasn't until I told her that all this was overstimulating, and in the way of the treatment, that she realized something had been amiss. Carol said she had the impression that something was wrong but couldn't quite put her finger on it.

Sarah's Story

Sarah was in group therapy with a clinician who encouraged her to begin training as a group therapist at the institute that he led. Within the first month at the institute, she was brought up short when she approached her group therapist in the staff lounge and was about to hand him a check for the past month's therapy sessions, when he said sharply, "Not here!" She felt rebuked. She had broken a boundary. But what did she know? She felt foolish and infantilized for have been scolded, but said nothing.

Murray's Story

Murray had been in a men's group in which there was a rule about no outside contact. Well into the treatment, the leader told Murray that he would make a good group therapist and encouraged Murray to study at the institute where the leader was an administrator. Once he began training at the institute, he ran into other men from the group who were in training there as well and became socially involved with them. Murray confided that it was an unreal feeling to see men, whose deepest and darkest secrets had been shared with him and his with them, hanging around the staff room, at staff meetings, in supervision groups, and at staff parties. Murray felt awkward and uncomfortable with the outside-group contact.

He worried how much of what he knew about them, or what they knew about him, would be revealed in this social setting. He was troubled about what might be revealed in group about his social persona. In other words, he fretted about being looped. This new world of blurred boundaries was confusing to him, and the new ground rules were never delineated. It became a game of trial and error.

Greg's Story

Greg was in two separate therapy groups that were led by his supervisor at the clinic where he worked as a therapist. He was in one group with the husband and in the other with the wife of a couple who were both colleagues of his at the clinic.

One night in group, the wife revealed that she had been unfaithful to her husband in a series of promiscuous liaisons with a variety of partners. Greg became very anxious and upset upon hearing this. *What was he supposed to do with this toxic information?* This was information that he would not have been privy to had he not been in group with her. He was in the untenable position of hearing this highly charged material of her betrayal and having to contain it. Greg was at a loss for words. What could he say, and to whom, without compromising the integrity of their therapy and his own?

He was furious with the senior leader for having been placed in this terrible bind. But Greg sat there in stunned silence. Not only was he conflicted about talking about all this in group, but at a loss to know with whom he could speak openly. Greg needed to talk to someone. He didn't feel safe speaking to his group therapist, who was also his individual therapist, because he no longer trusted his judgment. How could the therapist have done this to his patient/colleagues, and ultimately to himself? His behavior was potentially destructive and self-destructive. But how could this conflict be addressed in either of his two groups?

At that moment Greg felt paranoid and in danger. Group was no longer a safe place for him to say everything. It ceased to be a treatment group. From that time forward, he wanted out. But it took years for him to leave. Greg was in a double-bind. Not only did he feel protective of his group mates, but he felt strangely protective of and loyal to the leader. Greg thought that to reveal how he felt would jeopardize his therapist's role as the group leader. It also forced him to see the therapist in an unflattering light. As a clinician himself,

Greg was critical of the therapist's decision to treat both partners of a sexually acting-out couple. To whom did he owe his loyalty?

Greg thought to himself, *How could that SOB have compromised my treatment too?*" Greg realized that his therapist was not beyond placing his own needs ahead of his patients' needs. He wondered if it was for money or some other form of gratification that he did this. Greg hated him and thought that he was narcissistic, incompetent, arrogant, and greedy to have simultaneously destroyed the treatment of the three of them.

Greg found himself in a bizarre triangle. He was angry at himself for having trusted his leader's judgment to have put him in two treatment groups, and was also afraid of his angry impulse to divulge this in group. In vengeful fantasies toward the leader, he imagined blurting out what he knew about the wife in the husband's group. Just the thought of it filled him with great dread, guilt, and anxiety.

The compromise solution was to keep the secret and contain his own anxiety, all at the high cost of his feelings about the group therapist and the value of the treatment. There was no authentic group treatment. Once again we see a now familiar pattern in which the leader has created a topsy-turvy system in which power roles were reversed. The senior leader's practice more closely resembled a schizophrenic family, as described by R. D. Laing (1970), in which family members are not allowed to know what they know.

In this group therapy family, Greg held tremendous unwanted power that frightened him when he realized the havoc that he could wreak on the leader's practice, on the couple's relationship, and his own relationships in and out of the group therapy. Greg felt tacitly responsible for keeping the whole crazy system together by keeping his secret.

There were at least two secrets that he had to contain. The first was the details of the wife's extramarital behavior, and the other was the senior therapist's responsibility for breaching the wife's confidentiality and contaminating the group treatment for all of them. In blurring the boundaries, the leader had put everyone at risk, himself included. *What a fool he was,* Greg thought. *What the hell was he thinking, anyway?* Treatment was hopelessly confounded in this incestuous environment. For him to have exposed any of this, in either group, would have made him the potential target of scapegoating.

All these negative emotions were iatrogenic, in that they were created as a direct result of the senior leader's blatant disregard for appropriate boundaries and the potential harm done to confidentiality in an incestuous system in which members had complicated social relations with each other.

Leah's Story: Another Instance of Keeping a Secret

When I told Greg's story to an audience of group therapists, one colleague had a very different view of his dilemma; it was a 180-degree turn-around. She thought that I was naïve, and took umbrage with my notion that there was something untoward about the incestuous nature of interactions at these organizations. She said that it was known that when you're in group treatment with colleagues you will hear a lot of very personal, even disturbing information about them. Her solution was simply: Keep it to yourself. Don't gossip; don't talk to anyone about it, not even in therapy with your own institute-affiliated therapist. The intensity of her reaction was shocking. It seemed to me that she was suggesting that denial was a legitimate way to cope with the obstacles of these relationships and that she was very protective of the conspiracy of silence.

LEE KASSAN'S BOOK

Lee Kassan's (1996) *Shrink Rap* is a collection of interviews with clinicians about their experiences in practice. In the section on the clinician's experiences with patients who report substandard treatment with unethical therapists, there's a vignette of a group leader's egregious behavior that goes well beyond immoral.

To quote the clinician's patient report: "He [the group therapist] would have sexual intercourse with one of the female patients in front of the group…if patients didn't cooperate. . .they were fined huge sums of money. . .he was under indictment. . .moved to another country. . . and the group would meet. . .via phone and (he would) charge them for it. *After a while, the people in the group began to recognize that he was a charlatan"* (Kassan, 1996, pp.546-547, italics mine). It seems outrageous that group members accepted this behavior for even a minute. That it took members "a while" to figure out this man was corrupt is an extreme testament to the regressive nature of group. It also indicates the depth of some members' passivity and their childlike need to be taken care of, at any cost.

CONCLUSION

Life is messy. And as I have noted elsewhere (Pepper, 2014a), "we shall not cease from blurring boundaries in group psychotherapy (apologies to T.S. Eliot)." This seems particularly the case in the group treatment of group therapists themselves. In part, the pervasiveness of dual relationships at analytic group training institutes assures the status quo.

In this era of the dwindling supply of training candidates, financial austerity alone has created a panicked atmosphere of economic need in some of these institutes. The self-serving thinking of institute administrators was aptly, but I would assume inadvertently, stated by one clinician who panned an article that I submitted to a professional journal where he served as a reviewer. (See Chapter 3.)

The dangers of blurred boundaries will remain an issue for the group treatment of leaders-in-training, who will then pass the problem along onto the general population of group members. It is the premise of this book that the frame of the treatment is as important as theory and technique in understanding the healing power of group. In fact, it is my contention that without secure boundaries group treatment is diluted at best, and at worst it is contaminated. The treatment of group leaders may be the most contaminated treatment of all.

Epilogue

Some Thoughts about Betrayal in Group Psychotherapy

Dr. Anna Fels, in an article entitled "Great Betrayals," writes that the theme of betrayal is the subject of many memoirs. She muses that most people are not writers and do not have the option to "metabolize this toxic experience through the process of writing" (p. 9). I have been one of the fortunate ones. Over the last twenty-five years or so, I have done just that. I have sublimated the indignation of professional betrayal through writing.

It has been a challenge to portray myself objectively and take as much responsibility as I possibly can for my part. I never want to come across as a victim. In the first place, it's not true and in the second, I don't want to be dismissed as a complainer. I take full responsibility for my share of this unfolding drama.

Years ago when I first presented my story of deceit at the hands of an unscrupulous group therapist to a training group in which I participated, a woman member, whose name and face I don't recall, approached me at the end of the next meeting and handed me a Xeroxed copy of James Hillman's unpublished article entitled "Betrayal." I had never heard of him before, but after reading the article I realized that his brilliant essay would serve as a perfect metaphor for my own search, and the search of other group leaders, who are motivated to seek out the magical father.

Hillman begins the article with the story of a Jewish father who teaches his son a valuable life lesson—to be less afraid and have more courage. In the parable the father encourages his young son to jump from a high staircase into his arms. The fearful but trusting boy jumps successfully several times from increasing heights until the last trial when the father lets him fall flat on his face. After which the father warns (to paraphrase): "Never trust any man too much, particularly if he's your own father. The exact quote from Hillman is, "That will teach you: never trust a Jew, even if it's your own father" (Hillman, 1974, p. 63). It seems to me that the anti-Semitism of the parable detracts from the main point, so I changed the wording.

Hillman's point was that trust and betrayal are inextricably connected and are inherent to psychological life. He says the potentiality of betrayal is in built into any close and emotional intense relationship, such as that of parent and child, husband and wife, or even therapist and patient.

For instance, Hillman notes the sense of betrayal on the part of the patient whose analyst doesn't fully understand him or her; this can occur, as the psychoanalyst Jay Greenberg (1995) notes, even in its most benign yet still devastating form. Greenberg muses, in his writings about psychoanalysis, that the analysand is often disappointed by the analyst when the irrational, childlike, and magical hope is dashed that, simply by being a good patient, the analysis will serve as an amulet that protects from all emotional and physical hurt. It is a painful realization indeed that the analysis ultimately offers no protection from the universal betrayals of everyday life, such as the loss of a loved one, emotional instability, or the ravages of one's own aging.

On a more primal level, there is feeling of betrayal when the therapist's behavior obviates the prime dictum of the Hippocratic Oath: "Above all else, do no harm," as in the instance of the analyst who breaches confidentiality and reveals his patient's deepest secrets (Zur, 2009), and where the publications of clinical material by some psychotherapists include too much information in the case histories and patients' identities are exposed.

Hillman (1974) concludes that buried within the awareness of betrayal is a potential growth experience, where the betrayed has the opportunity to enter fully into adulthood and consciousness, through the mindfulness that no one can ever be fully trusted, not even oneself. He compares this experience to the biblical tale of Adam and Eve's expulsion from Eden.

In looking for the opportunity to live a charmed life, to be taken care of by an all-powerful and all-knowing father, perhaps unlike one's own biological progenitor, a neophyte group therapist might attach himself or herself to charismatic, brilliant, grandiose, and authoritarian leaders whose institutes more closely resemble religious cults than centers of learning (Temerlin & Temerlin, 1982). Ultimately, however, the blind trust of the initiate must be betrayed, as I have noted. Philip Slater (1974) points out that "sooner or later, all protection contracts eventually become protection rackets" (p. 89). In essence, the leader says: "I'll take care of you, but at a high cost; when I do, your soul belongs to me."

This is the same dynamic that Raubolt (2006) presents in his relationship to a charismatic but abusive training supervisor. It's a theme that I too described in Chapter 3 when I wrote, among other examples, about the deal that Bram Stoker's Dracula makes with his prey. He can only enter the souls of others who invite him in. That is his power. The irony is that there cannot be betrayal without the willingness to trust. And more to the point, there are no leaders without followers. So the question can be raised: Who has the power in any relationship? One might conclude that passivity is the ultimate form of control. Since not all who engage in dual relationships suffer ego dysfunction, there must be validity to the idea that personality plays a large role in this process.

Many of us group therapists, like many of our group members, want to be taken care of. It is not just our emotional, spiritual, and financial needs that are in question. On a deeper unconscious level we want to be taken care of in some unconditional and even supernatural way. We are looking for the "wonder rabbi" who will understand us at our core and who will even do magic. We're looking for the messiah.

There's an old story of a small town in Eastern Europe where a wonder rabbi appears one day and offers the townspeople protection from all evil, if they agree to follow him. Excited about this offer, the people ask the town's rabbi for his opinion. The rabbi offers this sagacious advice: "If someone offers protection from all the bad things in the world on the condition that he be followed, then don't follow him."

The Buddhists say that when the student is ready the teacher appears. Up to a point, this may be true. Ironically, my group therapist/supervisor once advised that, ultimately, we all must keep our own counsel. I believe he was right. For better or worse, we're all alone to struggle with our personal demons. The opportunity for unconditional acceptance starts at birth and lasts for the first several months of life. After that, the process of socialization and its qualified acceptances begin. When we finally give up looking, perhaps then the teacher appears. Pogo once said it quite well: "We have met the enemy and he is us" (Kelly, 1953).

Some years ago, I was on a plane seated next to a mother with a young child. As the plane descended for landing, the pressure on the child's ears began to hurt. In tears, the child begged his mother, "Mommy, make it stop." It's that kind of need that I am referring to.

The infantile wish to be cared for can interfere with the neophyte group leader's own personal development and, by osmosis, it can impede his or her willingness and ability to help group members learn to individuate. The prime goal of psychotherapy is to help patients understand the emotions that underlie their decisions, a seemingly simple task that is actually quite daunting. The group member's urge to regress, and the leader's impulse to gratify his or her own narcissism, are both so potent that it's like Ulysses' attempt to resist the sirens' song. We must all lash ourselves to the mast in order to avoid being dashed against the rocks.

My group therapist/supervisor, the one who encouraged me to do imagery therapy with my father, once told me that training to be a group therapist distills into this twisted adage: "You get your ass kicked and then you go out and kick someone else's ass." This turned out to be the understatement of the year but at the time it actually made sense to me.

As an ironic twist to my story, long after I left treatment with him, my group therapist/supervisor approached me and asked if he had done anything to precipitate my emotional breakdown. After years of his being defensive and insisting that it was entirely my fault, that it was my transference, he was finally taking responsibility for his part in this. When I said, "Why do you ask?" he told me, "Because someone else in my practice was going through the same thing." I felt moved as I told him that he hadn't protected me from his own mistakes. I became emotional because a long-buried, unmet need was finally being met. I had wanted him to ask me that question years before, so this was a bittersweet moment. In another poignant twist, he often told me that "the messiah always comes the day after we don't need him anymore."

And as a postscript, I never did get to train with Dr. Hyman Spotnitz. By the time I was ready to take on the biggest of the modern kahunas, he had retired, crazy red wig and all.

When writing about the pass-along effect as one of the seven dangers of blurred boundaries, I was including myself. After having been in a compromised treatment environment as a neophyte clinician, I learned about being a group therapist from my own group therapy. I thought that the role of group therapist was to run group members' lives, even making major real-life decisions for them.

It felt like culture shock when I entered a secure frame treatment milieu. I began therapy with someone who had a very clear sense of boundaries and realized that I had to relearn the role of a group therapist. Although I knew I needed it, I didn't know what to make of her unobtrusive ways. At the same time, I kept one foot in the Modern Analytic door.

Because I Need the Eggs

Richard Raubolt and colleagues (2006) have confirmed my observations both about the negative impact of supervision at group training institutes run by charismatic, brilliant, grandiose, authoritarian, and sadistic leaders, and about the neurotic needs of the trainees who willingly follow them (Pepper, 1990, 1991, 1992, 1997) but with one twist. At the time that I wrote those articles, I didn't tell the whole story. In fact, I may have left out the best part—my experiences training with Dr. X. and Dr. Y. weren't entirely bad.

They both taught various effective Modern Analytic techniques to resolve the negative transference with pre-oedipal group members. However, our relationships were conflicted, for both them and for me. For example, as much as Dr. X. could be wonderfully supportive and encouraging, he could also be verbally abusive.

On one occasion, he told me that my writing was at the cutting edge of our profession and that I had a "gothic mind." But on another, Dr. X. scolded me in group for having published an article critical of his institute. And when I objected to his advice to another member that seemed to me to be an unhealthy blurring of boundaries, he turned to her and said: "Be wary of obsessive-compulsive clinicians who insist on sterile boundaries in group." He called me a nut. It was a very mixed bag, indeed, a love-hate relationship between the two of us.

There was a time when I allowed myself to be vulnerable in the supervision group, and spoke of my worry that group members, in the groups that I ran, were angry with me all too often. I fretted that something was wrong with me. To my pleasant surprise, he was reassuring and said that my propensity to draw group members' rage was actually a talent.

For example, there was an occasion when I was conducting a workshop at a professional conference, coincidentally on the topic of working with difficult members in group therapy; some participants took an immediate dislike to me.

During my introductory remarks, I was lecturing on the thesis that the success of a group leader is dependent upon on the clinician's comfort managing aggression—both his and her own and that of the group—when, seemingly from nowhere, one male member took offense to my socks! Through clenched teeth and twitching cheek muscles, he said that he hated them and he would never be in group therapy with a leader who wore socks like that (the socks were black with thin gray stripes—and for the record, *I was wearing shoes*, black loafers to be exact).

Unbelievably, another male attendee chimed in and lambasted me for wearing a pink bowtie. He said that I looked "haughty." Who knows what transferences were activated in this group! In any case, I had planned to do a demonstration group later on in the workshop to show how I work with aggression but I didn't have to wait. It was happening right there in front of us! And so the work with difficult members was off and running.

Dr. X. told me that this quality was a gift; an asset he said, for a group therapist. He had put a positive spin on an aspect of my personality that had me worried. I began to think that perhaps I was a natural group therapist after all.

My Book Resistance

After Dr. X. died, I joined another modern analytic supervision group with Dr. Y. When I first met him, I thought he was the best at the technique known as *joining*[1] ; actually I thought that he was too good at it. I was put off by what I experienced as an act, a mask that seemed insincere. Over the years, I had a change of heart toward him, particularly when he protected me in a workshop that he ran where several of the women tried to kill me off right from the start.

When I presented my resistance to writing this book to Dr.Y.'s group, he asked me if my father would have been supportive of such a project. I didn't have to think about it. Yes, he would, but it wasn't until after *my professional fathers* had died that I realized that it might be my *symbolic* fathers who would have had a problem with it. I had put myself in the crazy adolescent position of writing critically about them and then expected to be loved for it.

Oscar Wilde once famously said, "Be careful what you wish for, you might get it." When my first article was accepted for publication, I went into a paranoid panic. I understood the fear that I described in Chapter 6 of those clinicians who changed their minds about my publishing the interviews that I had with them.

Finally, I was to expose my own struggle with the conspiracy of silence, and I was now apprehensive of what might ensue as a result. I had taken on my fathers and I awaited their retaliation. When it didn't come, I was almost disappointed.

In fact, I wanted their praise for having taken them on. That didn't come either. During the student uprisings of the '60s at Columbia University, the sociology professor Dr. Amatai Etzioni reported that one dissident leader approached him after a takeover of a building and said, "Didn't I do good?" That could have been me, the adolescent rebel looking for his father's approval.

I felt hurt when a group member, Morris, accused me, in front of the group, of being a Judas. I got nervous. *Here it comes*, I thought. But Henry, another group member, came to my defense and said, "Well, at least he didn't mention any names!" The truth is, emotional separation always breeds unease, even if it's for the best. Talking about boundary issues always raised my anxiety, as it did for those who heard me speak.

So naturally, I was quite anxious about the prospect of presenting my first workshop ever, "Blurred Boundaries in Group Psychotherapy," at an American Group Psychotherapy Association meeting in Atlanta, Georgia, in 1996. I was so nervous that I almost missed my own presentation. Thankfully, part of my unconscious mind was on my side and I showed up on time in spite of myself.

The meeting was to begin at 9 a.m. but for some reason I thought it was to begin at noon. In order to be fully prepared, however, I decided to go to the room three hours early to set it up and ready the Power Point. When I arrived, a little before nine, I got a surprise: *the participants were all in their seats, ready to begin*. I was shocked to see them, and when I asked them what they were all doing there so early, they were incredulous. One said, "We're only five minutes early!" I acted as if I were joking but thanked my lucky stars that I realized my mistake. I was less ambivalent about presenting than I thought. I didn't miss a beat and quipped, "Thank you for welcoming me, Dr. Pepper, to Atlanta, the home of Coca-Cola."

After the presentation ended I was in a daze. It went well, although one man accused me of running a "pity party." I let that remark go, and ran out of the hotel to catch a shuttle van to the airport for my flight back to New York. Outside the hotel lobby was a minivan, like the one that brought me to the conference, double-parked with a car full of people ready to go. I thought it was the free shuttle so I jumped in and the van took off. After a half-hour drive, I noticed that we hadn't seen any highway signs to the airport, so I asked the driver why not. He said that the van was traveling in the opposite direction, to the Leibowitz Bar Mitzvah. I had jumped into the wrong van! I asked him to turn around and take me back. He couldn't do that. The bar mitzvah guests were hysterical. They thought it was hilarious but I was in a panic about missing my flight. One woman invited me to join them; but I declined, saying that I couldn't—I didn't bring a gift! The driver dropped me at the nearest hotel and I had to pay a cab to drive me back to the airport.

A Final Thought

I am not naïve enough to think that group training institutes will change their attitude toward dual relationships simply because I have written about them. I believe that the best that can be hoped for is that the professional organizations of group psychotherapy will continue to offer members an opportunity to talk about their experiences with blurred boundaries, particularly if group members are not free to openly discuss these matters either in their own group treatments or at the institutes where they are in training.

In Chapter 3, I wrote about the director who had invited me to sit in as an ethics consultant at an organizational meeting of the institute that he was forming. He believed that if it were good enough for him to have been trained in a blurred boundary environment, it was good enough for his students. But this is not the whole story.

Despite the fact that he dismissed my concerns about dual relationships, he asked me to participate in the organization in the capacity of chairman of the ethics committee. It was a seductive offer and I was initially flattered. But after consulting with my new supervisor, Gerry Appel, I decided against it.

Gerry wisely advised that no one was going to listen to the advice of Robert Pepper without the director's unconditional 100 percent backing; otherwise my time and energy would be wasted and I would most likely wind up feeling exploited and foolish. Gerry warned that I could be used as window dressing, allowing the director to say to the world, "See, we have an ethics committee with an expert in the field as our chairman." *But with no one in the organization taking me seriously*, I decided that my efforts would be most effective as an outsider.

The best-case scenario for the resolution of harm done to group members through altered frame therapy is for professional organizations to sponsor open sessions, workshops, and lectures on the subject. Just as an external source of validation of her perceptions saved the wife in *Gaslight* from being driven mad, so too can group therapists be spared the negative effects of contaminated treatment milieus.

It doesn't seem likely that in the near future, many of the institutes and the group leaders that train neophyte group therapists through the establishment of dual relationships will change their ways of conducting therapy. There are potent intrapersonal, interpersonal, and organizational forces in place that will sustain the status quo for many years to come. Inertia is a potent force to be reckoned with.

The emotional gratification and financial investment alone are highly resistant to change. But at the very least, let's keep talking about it. Giving clinicians the opportunity to share their experiences with this endemic problem will go a long way toward stabilizing at-risk members of the profession.

NOTE

1. First introduced by Robert Lindner in his book, *The Fifty Minute Hour*, in the chapter entitled, "The Jet-Propelled Couch," the term refers to an intervention in which the clinician doesn't oppose the patient's distorted thinking but instead goes along with it.

References

American Group Psychotherapy Association (1999). Ethical guidelines for group therapists. *The Group Circle (newsletter)*, New York: Author.

American Psychological Association (1992). *The ethical standards of psychologists*. Washington, DC: American Psychological Association.

American Psychological Association (2002). *The ethical standards of psychologists*. Washington, DC: American Psychological Association.

Aronson, M. (1977). The unique advantages of analytic group therapy in middle and later phases of the therapeutic process. Wolberg, R., Aronson, M.L. (Ed.) *Group therapy 1977: an overview*, 36–46. New York: Stratton Intercontinental Medical Book Corp.

Asch, S. (1951). Effects of group pressure upon the modification and distortions of judgment. In H. Guetzkow (Ed.) *Groups, Leadership and Men*, 177-190. Pittsburgh: Carnegie Press.

Bateson, G., Jackson, D. , Haley, J., & Weakland, D. (1956). Toward a theory of schizophrenia. *Behavioral Science* , Vol. 1. No.4, 151–164.

Bazilian, S. E. (1993). Iatrogenic blocks to therapeutic progress; A study of countertransference resistances. *Modern Psychoanalysis*, *18*(2). 157–178.

Brothers, D. (2003). Clutching at certainty: Thoughts on the coercive grip of cult–like groups. *GROUP, 27*(2/3), 79–88.

Calef, V., & Weinshel, E. (1981). Some clinical consequences of introjection: Gaslighting. *Psychoanalytic Quarterly*, *50*, 44–66.

Carroll, L (2004). *Alice in wonderland.* New York: Barnes & Noble Books.

Chessick, R. (1974). *The technique and practice of intensive psychotherapy.* New York: Jason Aronson.

Clinical Social Work Federation (1997). Code of ethics. Arlington, VA: Clinical Social Work Federation.

DeSteno, D. (2014). Stop trusting yourself. *The New York Times: Review of the Week* (January 19), 12.

Dorpat, T. (1985). *Defense and denial in the therapeutic situation*. New York: Jason Aronson.

Dorpat, T. (1996). *Gaslighting, the double whammy, interrogation and other methods of covert control in psychotherapy and analysis.* Northvale, NJ: Jason Aronson.

Dorpat, T. (2006). Overt methods of interpersonal control. In R. Raubolt (Ed.) *Power games*. New York: Other Press. 93–118.

Dulchin, J., & Siegal, A. (1982). The ambiguity of confidentiality in a psychoanalytic institute. *Psychiatry, 45*(1), 27–37.

Dutton, D. & Painter, S. L. (1986 June). Traumatic bonding and the battered wife. *Psychology Today*, 18.

Fels, A. (2013). Great betrayals. *New York Times* (October 6), 9.

Fenichel, O. (1974). *The psychoanalytic theory of neurosis* (rev. ed.). New York: Norton.
Festinger, L., Riecken, H. W., & Schacter, S. (1956). *When prophecy fails.* Minneapolis, MN: University of Minnesota Press.
Freud, S. (1910). *The future prospects of psych-analytic theory.* 11, 139.
Freud, S. (1913). Papers on technique: On beginning treatment. Standard edition.12, 121.
Freud, S. (1961). On psychoanalysis. *Standard Edition, 12*, 207–211.
Freud, S. (1921). *Group Psychology and the analysis of the ego. Standard edition.* Vol. 18, 105.
Fromm, E. (1941). *Escape from freedom.* New York: Henry Holt and Company.
Gabbard, G. O., & Lester, E. (1995). *Boundaries and boundary violations in psychoanalysis.* Washington, DC: American Psychiatric Publishing.
Gabbard, G. O. (2005). *Psychodynamic psychiatry in clinical practice.* (4th ed.). New York: American Psychiatric Press.
Gans, J. (1992). Money and psychodynamic group psychotherapy. *International Journal of Group Psychotherapy, 42*(2), 133–152.
Gans, J. (2014). What an understanding of the dynamics of gossip has to teach about group dynamics and group leadership. *International Journal of Group Psychotherapy, 64*(1), 5–22.
Giles, T. R. (1993). *Managed health care: A guide for practitioners, employers and hospital administrators.* Boston: Allyn & Bacon.
Gleick, J. (1986). *Chaos: Making a new science.* New York: Penguin Books.
Goffman, E. (1961). *Asylums.* New York: Anchor Books.
Goleman, D. (1985). *Vital lies, simple truths.* New York: Simon and Schuster.
Greenberg, J. (1995). Editorial. *Contemporary Psychoanalysis,* 31(5), 1.
Harwood, I. (1998). Can group analysis/psychotherapy provide a wide angle lens for self-psychology? In *Self experiences in group intersubjectivity and self psychological pathways to human understanding* (155–174). London and Philadelphia: Jessica Kingsley.
Hillman, J. (1974). Betrayal. Unpublished article.
Kassan, L. D. (1996). *Shrink rap.* Northvale, NJ: Jason Aronson.
Kassan, L. D. (2010). *Peer supervision: How they work and why you need one.* Lanham, MD: Jason Aronson.
Kelly, W. (1953). *The Pogo Papers.* New York: Simon & Schuster.
Kirsner, D. (2000). *Unfree associations.* London: Process Press.
Kramer, E. (1987). The analyst's resolution of revenge resulting from the treatment of his parents. *Modern Psychoanalysis, 12*(2), 207–219.
Laing, R. D. (1970). *Knots.* New York: Pantheon.
Langs, R. (1977) *The therapeutic interaction: A synthesis.* New York: Jason Aronson.
Langs, R. (1982). *The psychotherapeutic conspiracy.* New York: Jason Aronson.
Langs, R. (1989). *Rating your psychotherapist.* New York: Henry Holt.
Lewis, M. (2009). *Panic.* New York: Norton.
Liegner, E. (1984). Countertransference in the treatment of friends and relatives. *Modern Psychoanalysis, 9*(2), 157–169.
Lindner, R. (1999). *The fifty-minute hour.* New York: Other Press.
Livingston, M. (2006). Discussion: Vulnerability, charisma, and trauma in the training experience. In R. Raubolt (Ed.) *Power games* (pp. 83–92). New York: Other Press.
Maeder, T. (1989). Wounded healers. *The Atlantic* (January). 37–47.
Maroda, K. (1999). *Seduction, surrender, and transformation: Emotional engagement in the analytic process.* London: Analytic Press.
Maroda, K. (2000). Controversial discussions: Use of the home office. *Psychologist Psychoanalyst, 20*(2), 20–21.
Michels, R. (1983). Contemporary psychoanalytic views of interpretation. In L. Grinspoon, (Ed): *Psychiatry update: The American Psychiatric Association Review, 11*, 61–70.
Milgram, S. (1963). Behavioral study of obedience. *Journal of Abnormal Psychology, 67*(4), 371–378.
Moreno, J. K. (2007). Scapegoating in group psychotherapy. *International Journal of Group Psychotherapy,* 57(1), 93–104.
Mullan, H. (1987). The ethical foundations of group psychotherapy. *International Journal of Group Psychotherapy, 37*(3), 403–416.

Neurath, P. M. (2005). *The Society of Terror.* (N. Stehr & C. Flck, Eds.): Boulder, Co.: Paradigm Press.
Novick, J. & Novick, K. (1996). *Fearful symmetry.* Northvale, NJ: Jason Aronson.
Ormont, L. (1974). The treatment of pre–oedipal resistance in group psychotherapy. *Psychoanalytic Review. 61*(3), 429–441.
Ormont, L. (2001). *The technique of group treatment.* (L. B. Furgeri, Ed.), Madison, CT: Psychosocial Press.
Pepper, R. (1989). Therapist's transparency and multiple role relations. *International Journal of Group Psychotherapy, 39*(1), 131–132.
Pepper, R. (1990). When transference isn't transference: Iatrogenesis of multiple role relations between practicing therapists. *Journal of Contemporary Psychotherapy, 20*(3), 141–153.
Pepper, R. (1991). The senior therapist's grandiosity: clinical and ethical consequences of merging multiple roles. *Journal of Contemporary Psychotherapy, 21*(1), 53–70.
Pepper, R. (1992). Psychoanalytic training institutes as cults: An example of entropy. *Journal of Contemporary Psychotherapy, 22*(1), 35–42.
Pepper, R. (1996). The omnipotent clinician: A potential source of iatrogenesis. *Journal of Contemporary Psychotherapy, 26*(3), 287–294.
Pepper, R. (1997). Treatment with unethical practitioners: Caveat emptor. *Journal of Contemporary Psychotherapy, 27*(3), 215–223.
Pepper, R. (2001a). About Dr. Zur's: "Out of office experience" article. *The Independent Practitioner. 21*(3). 201–202.
Pepper, R. (2001b). The leader's oral greed and gaslighting in group psychotherapy. *Group Psychologist, 2*(3), 41–43.
Pepper, R. (2002). Emotional incest in group psychotherapy. *International Journal of Group Psychotherapy, 52*(2), 285–294.
Pepper, R. (2003a). Raising fees and informed consent in group psychotherapy. *The Group Circle,* October/November. Newsletter.
Pepper, R. (2003b). Be it ever so humble…the controversial issue of psychotherapy groups in the home office setting. *GROUP, 27*(1), 41–52.
Pepper, R. (2004). Confidentiality and dual relationships in group psychotherapy. *International Journal of Group Psychotherapy, 54*(1), 103–114.
Pepper, R. (2004). Raising group fees: some ethical and clinical implications. *Journal of Contemporary Psychotherapy, 34*(2), 141-152.
Pepper, R. (2007). Too close for comfort: the impact of dual relationships on group therapy and group therapy training. *International Journal of Group Psychotherapy, 57*(1), 13–23.
Pepper, R. (2013). Stirring the pot: some clinical and ethical implications of blurred boundaries. *GROUP, 37* (2), 135–146.
Pepper, R. (2014). Group lite: The bane of the group leader's own group treatment—blurred boundaries. *GROUP, 38*(1), 55–69.
Pepper, R. (2014b). Response to Stone. *GROUP.* 38(2), 171-172.
Phillips, D. (2013). What happened to confidentiality? *The Clinician: The Newsletter of the New York State Society for Clinical Social Workers*, *44*(2), 4, 18.
Postman, N., & Weingartner, C. (1969) *Teaching as a subversive activity.* New York: Delacorte Press.
Racker, H. (1987). *Transference and countertransference.* Madison, CT: International Universities Press.
Raubolt, R. (2003). Attack on the self: Charismatic leadership and authoritarian group supervision. *Group, 27*(2/3), 65–78.
Raubolt, R. (2006). Coerced discipleship: indoctrination masquerading as training in psychotherapy. In R. Raubolt (Ed.), *Power games* (169–186). New York: Other Press.
Richard, A. (2006). A therapist's initiatory journey through submission in a coercive training program. In R. Raubolt (Ed.) *Power games* (11–36). New York: Other Press.
Roazen, P. (1974). *Freud and his followers*. New York: Meridian Press.
Rosenthal, L. (1987). *Resolving resistance in group psychotherapy.* Northvale, NJ: Jason Aronson.

Rosenthal, L. (1992) The new member: Infanticide in group psychotherapy. *International Journal of Group Psychotherapy, 42*(2), 277–286.
Scheidlinger, S. (1982). Presidential address: on scapegoating in group psychotherapy. *International Journal of Group Psychotherapy, 32*(2), 131–143.
Scharf, M. (1987). *Intimate partners.* New York: Random House.
Schumann, E. P. (1999). Group dynamics. *Psychology: A Journal of Human Behavior, 36*(3–4), 24.
Schumann, E. P. (2007). Marketing psychotherapeutic expertise. *Annals of Modern Psychoanalysis, 3*(1), 83–87.
Sedgwick, D. (1994). *The Wounded Healer.* London: Routledge Press.
Simonton, O. C., Matthews–Simonton, K.S., & Sparks, T. F. (1980). Psychological intervention in the treatment of cancer. *Psychosomatics, 3*, 226–230.
Slater, P. (1974). *Earthwalk.* New York: Doubleday.
Slater, P. (1977). *Footholds.* Boston: Beacon Press.
Slochower, J. (2014). *Psychoanalytic collisions (2 nd ed.).* New York: Routledge.
Spotnitz, H. (1976*). Psychotherapy of pre-oedipal conditions.* New York: Jason Aronson.
Stoker, B. (1981). Stade, G. Introduction to Bram Stoker's *Dracula* (first published in 1897). New York: Bantam Books.
Stone, W.(2014) Thinking about our work: Case presentations. *GROUP.* 38(2), 153-154.
Temerlin, J., & Temerlin, M. (1982). Psychotherapy cults: An iatrogenic perversion. *Psychotherapy: Theory, Research, Practice, 31*(7), 86.
Vinogradov, S. & Yalom, I. (1989). *Group psychotherapy.* Washington, DC: American Psychiatric Press.
Weinberg, G. (1990). *The taboo scarf.* New York: St. Martin's Press.
Weinberg, G. (1993). *Nearer the heart's desire.* New York: Penguin Books.
West, M., & Livesley, W. (1986). Therapist transparency and the frame for group psychotherapy. *International Journal of Group Psychotherapy. 36*(1), 5–19.
Yalom, I. (1985). *The theory and practice of group psychotherapy.* New York: Basic Books.
Yalom, I. & Leszcz, M. (2005). *The theory and practice of group psychotherapy.* New York: Basic Books.
Zimbardo, P. (2007). *The lucifer effect.* New York: Random House.
Zur, O. (2001a). Out of the office experience: When crossing office boundaries and engaging in dual relationships are clinically ethical and sound. *Independent Practitioner, 21*(1), 96–100.
Zur, O. (2001b). On analysis, transference and dual relationships: A rejoinder to Dr. Pepper. *Independent Practitioner, 21*(3), 201–204.
Zur, O. (2009). *Boundaries in psychotherapy: Ethical and clinical explorations.* Washington, DC: American Psychological Association.

Subject Index

Name Index

About the Author

Robert S. Pepper has been leading analytic psychotherapy groups for over thirty-five years. Currently, he runs six (6) ongoing transference groups in his private practice in Forest Hills, New York. He is the director of education and training of the Long Island Institute for Mental Health, Rego Park, New York. Dr. Pepper is also an adjunct professor of Behavioral Science at the Metro Campus of the New York Institute of Technology in Manhattan. He is the author of numerous articles on ethics and boundaries in group psychotherapy. In his free time, Dr. Pepper enjoys hanging out with his grandchildren, Sydney and CJ, and sailing his sloop, the *PepperPot*, on the Great South Bay of Long Island. He lives on the Upper Westside of Manhattan with his fiancée, Lois, and their dog, "Molly."

CPSIA information can be obtained at www.ICGtesting.com
Printed in the USA
BVOW05*1219110914

366158BV00003B/7/P

9 781442 244016